Your Private Pilot's Licence

You too can be a pilot – that is the simple message of this friendly but authoritative little volume. In it you are put in the command seat of an aeroplane and shown what actually happens in the air, with an experienced instructor taking you step by step through the practical side of learning to fly and gaining a Private Pilot's Licence. It is a commonsense approach to the most recurrent problems of the student pilot, which gives you the chance to understand at home the questions you forgot to ask during your lessons.

Included are the practical use of the radio, a detailed description of how to use the computer when working out a cross country flight plan, use of the VOR, setting the altimeter, an actual radio failure, how to regain and maintain control in cloud, followed by a Surveillance Radar Approach. At the end of the book, guidelines are given for taking the written examinations and the flight test.

Betty Cones learned to fly on Tiger Moths in the early Fifties, while she was an air stewardess with British European Airways. She later worked for the Air Ministry. After some years in the United States, where she flew extensively, she returned to England and helped to found the British Section of the international organisation of women pilots known as The Ninety Nines. She worked for five years at the College of Air Traffic Control before becoming a flying instructor at Hurn, Hampshire. Apart from her British ratings, she holds an American Commercial Pilot's Licence and Instrument Rating.

YOUR
PRIVATE
PILOT'S
LICENCE

BETTY CONES

PITMAN

PITMAN PUBLISHING LIMITED
39 Parker Street, London WC2B 5PB

Associated Companies
Copp Clark Limited, Toronto
Fearon-Pitman Publishers Inc, Belmont, California
Pitman Publishing New Zealand Ltd, Wellington
Pitman Publishing Pty Ltd, Melbourne

Text set in 10/12 pt VIP Sabon, printed by photolithography, and bound in
Great Britain at The Pitman Press, Bath

ISBN 0 273 01190 1

Contents

1 The start

So you want to learn to fly. You're crazy, of course, but let's look at how to get started.

First, brace yourself for the expense involved. The cost of flying lessons varies from club to club, but you should reckon on a minimum outlay of £500 for a British Private Pilot's course, usually broken up into payments after each flight. If you are not put off by the cost, once you have started, try to book regular lessons, so that you remember things more easily and avoid extra hours and money in revision.

You will have to find a flying school relatively close to your area, for with fuel the price it is today, there's little point in travelling many miles. However, if you do join a club some distance away, it is advisable to telephone before starting out, so that you don't have a wasted journey due to unflyable weather.

As flying schools need an airport, this is a good place to make enquiries. If possible, go to a school which is approved by the Civil Aviation Authority. If all goes well, you could have your licence after thirty-five hours, provided you complete the training within a period of six months. If you exceed this time period, or if you go to a non-approved school, you will need a minimum of forty hours before becoming eligible to take the test. With the expense involved, those extra five hours matter.

Before joining the flying club you will need to have a

medical check up with a doctor who is authorised to give examinations by the Civil Aviation Authority. The instructors or office staff at the club of your choice will be able to give you the name and address of such a doctor and you can then make an appointment with him. Among other things, he will examine you for heart, eyesight, blood pressure and hearing. Although it gives you an edge if you can see, don't be put off by the eyesight test, for your vision may well be corrected with glasses to acceptable limits. If the doctor decides you are healthy, you will be issued with a medical certificate. This is needed before you are allowed to fly by yourself (solo).

The next step is to apply for membership of the flying club and you will usually have to fill in an application form. Once accepted, you can expect to pay an initial entrance fee, and thereafter an annual membership subscription. Generally these are not too prohibitive. At most clubs you can take out a 'family membership' so that your wife (or husband) and children may enjoy the facilities of the club too.

You would be well advised to buy one or two of the excellent books on flying training, as there are various ground subjects you will need to understand for your written examinations at the end of the course. If you start reading the books early, you will absorb some of the material and help yourself with the flying, which is more useful than 'cramming' at the end.

The written examinations cover Navigation, Meteorology, Aviation Law, Airframes and Engines and how the aircraft instruments work. Don't write yourself off too soon, as the knowledge you are expected to have for a Private Pilot's examination at the end of thirty-five hours' training is not that required by a veteran Jumbo Jet pilot. Your instructor will recommend which books to buy and tell you how much you need to exercise your brain – and his.

You will need a log book for recording your flying hours, an aeronautical map, aviation computer, protractor, plotter, pencil – and rubber. These can generally be bought at the flying club.

This book is intended to go over some of the points in each of your lessons that you might not have fully understood, or forgot to query with your instructor before leaving for home, or maybe didn't like to ask about again. If you knew it all, you wouldn't be learning to fly in the first place, so never hesitate to ask, however stupid you feel. It could be that your instructor doesn't know the answers either, (he's human too), but he will certainly find out. Most instructors are highly approachable, having been through the same thing themselves. Remember, they are there to help you.

For our example aeroplane we will use a Cessna 150, which is a two-seater trainer widely used in club flying, and where it is necessary to illustrate a point, we will fly out of Hurn Airport, which has several runways and excellent Air Traffic Control. Substitute your own airport and the aircraft you fly when speeds and runway directions are mentioned.

Right, let's get started —

2 Air experience

In this lesson you can relax and enjoy getting used to the sensation of flying in a small aeroplane. You are not expected to remember much but try to look interested now and again, just to give your instructor hope for the future.

You will be shown how to strap yourself in and how to adjust the seat so that your feet can reach the rudder pedals and brakes easily. On most light aeroplanes the brakes are on the top part of the rudder pedals, so to use them, lift your heels off the floor and depress the brakes with the ball of each foot. You will sit in the left hand seat, for this is the 'Pilot-in-Command' seat for which you are training.

You will fly round the local area for about forty minutes and your instructor will point out distinctive landmarks and any restricted or prohibited areas in the vicinity. Take a look at your map to see how these are shown for they will be useful to remember. Always take the map with you, even for a short flight. If the weather deteriorated unexpectedly or your airport was closed for some reason, you would need it to find your way to another airfield.

You will probably fly the aeroplane, and the instructor will keep a beady eye on you. He will point out the Altimeter, which measures altitude or height, and the Airspeed Indicator. Try to remember the position of the aircraft nose in relation to the outside horizon, as it will be helpful to you a couple of lessons from now.

You will hear your instructor using the radio and apparently understanding that garbled noise coming back. Don't let this concern you. The radio will become quite straightforward with a bit of practice and it is the least of your worries at this stage.

After landing you will be shown how to fill in and complete the authorisation sheets, and how to make the first entry in your log book. Before you took off you may not have noticed your instructor 'booking out' with Air Traffic Control, but he will have done so, for it is a legal requirement to 'furnish brief details of the intended flight'. This is not the same as filing a flight plan – take a look at your aviation law book. Jot down the telephone numbers of Flight Clearance and the Meteorological Office for future reference.

The NOTAMS (Notices to Airmen) and details of Royal Flights will usually be displayed on a notice board, along with the current weather forecast for your area. Your instructor will explain how to use all the reference books and available information as you go through your training. You will be introduced to a massive tome known as the 'Air Pilot',* which has baffled many a pilot before you, so persevere –

* *Sections of the Air Pilot*
  AGA – Aerodromes and Ground Aids
  COM – Communications
  RAC – Rules of the Air and Air Traffic Control
  MET – Meteorology
  FAL – Facilitation
  SAR – Search and Rescue
  MAP – Maps and Charts
  GEN – General

3 Pre-flight

This inspection of the aircraft may have been covered with you before your first flight, but if not, rest assured that your instructor had satisfied himself that the aeroplane was in a fit state to fly before he took you (and himself) up in it.

From now on you will be expected to carry out a pre-flight inspection, for you will eventually assume responsibility before taking up passengers.

A normal inspection can be done quickly and efficiently – five to ten minutes should be sufficient. If you would like a check list, ask your instructor to show you the aircraft handbook and you will be able to copy it out.

Although different makes of aeroplanes have somewhat different layouts, there are basics to any pre-flight inspection. Here are the necessary items to be covered on a Cessna 150:

Check position of aircraft
As you walk up, make sure it is parked in a sensible place so that when you start the engine, the slipstream from the propeller won't throw loose grit on to other aeroplanes parked nearby or into the engineers' tea in the hangar.

Check that all surfaces are free of frost
Even a thin film of frost will seriously affect the 'lift' of the aircraft, so if there has been a cold snap overnight and the

aeroplanes have been left outside, prepare yourself for a rub down job before attempting to fly.

Place chocks under the wheels
Advisable, but don't forget to remove them before starting the engine, or you'll never get off the ground.

Check magneto switches OFF
Even with the master switch in the OFF position, it is possible to start the engine, so always be very careful about this. Do not assume that the student who has just taxyed in and closed down has also turned the switches to the OFF position.

Turn master switch ON

Switch pitot heat ON

Lower electric flaps (or manual flaps)

Switch rotating beacon ON
Check outside aeroplane to see that the beacon is operating on top of the tail fin.

Switch rotating beacon OFF

Check pitot tube
This is the elbow-shaped tube with a small hole in the tip of it, located under the port wing. Check that it is clear of obstructions and gently feel the tube to see if the electric heating element is starting to warm up — it takes a few moments.

Turn pitot heat OFF
Don't forget this, or you might overheat the element while you are stationary on the ground. The pitot heat check would not normally be necessary for you so early in your training, as you would not expect to be flying in conditions where ice might stick to the pitot tube, but it's as well to know the correct way to test that the element is functioning properly.

Electric gyro check
With the master switch on, you should be able to hear the running up of the electrically operated gyro for the turn needle. The artificial horizon and the directional gyro are also gyro instruments, but on this aeroplane they work through suction from an engine driven vacuum pump, and will not start to operate until the engine is running, even then taking a few minutes to reach their correct rotor speed.

Check fuel contents, then turn Master switch OFF
Always check that the fuel filler caps are secure after refuelling. Ask your instructor the fuel octane rating for your aircraft. Not only are you likely to get a question on this in one of your tests, but more important, it is something you need to know if you are planning a cross country flight and there is a possibility of having to re-fuel. You can find out the fuel available at other airfields by looking in the AGA section of the Air Pilot. Whenever possible, try to refuel after a flight and avoid leaving the aircraft with nearly empty tanks, which might allow condensation to form. Most aeroplanes are fitted with a 'quick drain' knob, and before the first flight of the day it is a good practice to drain off a small amount of fuel to check for the possible presence of water – being heavier than fuel, this will sink to the bottom of the tank. At most flying schools, the instructors or engineers will do this check before the aeroplane starts its day's work, but it is necessary for you to know where the drain is located. Continuing with the pre-flight.

Remove control lock and put it in the locker
This is the metal flag which is threaded through holes in the control column to lock the ailerons when the aircraft is left unattended.

Check static vent
This is the small round circle with a hole in the centre, located on the port side of the forward fuselage on the Cessna 150. Make sure the hole is clear of mud, paint, polish and ice. If you have started reading those books, you'll remember that the difference in pressures received from the static vent and the pitot tube give you the airspeed reading. The static vent also gives you pressure for the altimeter and the vertical speed indicator.

If you have difficulty remembering which is port and which is starboard, 'there's a little red port left' may help. Red is the colour of the navigation light on the tip of the port (left) wing and green is the colour on the starboard (right) wing. If a mnemonic helps you to remember something, use it. Make your own up, however ridiculous, but don't make the memory aid so complicated that you have more trouble remembering it than the thing you want to remember.

Check engine cowling
Secure, and no loose rivets

Check windscreen clear
You want everything going for you when you are in the aeroplane and it helps if you can see out, so don't take too many flies and bugs along for the ride. Those birds are a little indiscriminate too.

Check nosewheel conditions
Without a gauge it is difficult to tell if the exact amount of pressure is in the tyre, but you certainly need some air if it is sitting on its rim. Check that you have approximately 'four fingers' of oleo extension on the nose wheel strut and that all the nuts and bolts are secure.

Exhaust ports
Check for security.

Propeller
Check for nicks and cracks and for security. On the first flight of the day it is a good practice to pull the propeller through two or three times by hand – double check on those magneto switches first. This helps to loosen congealed oil and saves wear and tear on the battery when starting. On American aeroplanes, (such as the Cessna 150), the propeller turns in a clockwise direction, looking at it from the pilot's seat, and on some British aeroplanes it turns in an anti-clockwise direction.

Check air intakes clear
Make sure nothing has been stuffed into the cavities above the propeller, such as empty (or full) beer cans or newspapers. It isn't very probable while you are at the flying school, but people are thoughtless and this check is important if you take the aeroplane away for a day and leave it unattended for a while. Be prepared to find the makings of a bird's nest in that nice warm spot over the engine. Check the carburettor air intake, (that square mesh screen under the propeller), for bugs and obstructions.

Check oil contents
Lift the engine access flap on the starboard side of the engine and unscrew (anticlockwise) the oil filler cap. Capacity is five imperial quarts. If the engine is still warm from a previous flight, all the oil will not yet have returned to the sump, but you should not take off with less than four quarts. Secure the oil cap firmly.

Operate fuel strainer
First flight of day and after refuelling. One or two seconds

should suffice, so don't waste it. Make sure valve is properly closed again.

Check that you have an engine
It should be in good condition. You are not expected to be mechanically clever but it would be reasonable to query broken wires and gushing oil, or a badly corroded battery.

Close access flap and secure

Check security of starboard cowling

Check starboard windscreen for bugs
It's only your instructor who is sitting this side so don't pamper him. When you take the test, the Examiner will be in this seat and that's a different matter.

Starboard wing
Check cabin fresh air intake clear – (top of the wing next to the windscreen).

Look along the leading edge of the wing for bad dents or damage and check that the navigation light on the wing tip is unbroken and the correct colour – remember?

Lift up the aileron, which is hinged at the back of the wing just round the corner from the navigation light and visually check the hinges for security. Avoid putting your fingers in the slot to check the bolts as a helpful friend checking the port wing at the same time could cause you pain – when one aileron moves up, the other moves down.

Check the flaps for security.

Check security of the inspection panels under the wing.

Starboard undercarriage
Check for proper inflation and general condition of tyre. Make sure there are no hydraulic leaks from the tube running down the strut. Check for 'creep' – there is usually a painted mark on the tyre and on the rim and these should be aligned. If the tyre is creeping round the wheel rim, the valve might be damaged.

Open starboard cabin door
Check that the fire extinguisher is in place – you can see it easily from this side, to the left of where your left leg will be. The arrow should be pointing within the small white triangle on the dial if it is properly charged. If you ever have to use it for a small fire in the cabin – perhaps caused by a careless passenger dropping a cigarette – your vision will momentarily

be obscured by a powder-like snow. It is non-toxic and will clear quite quickly through the fresh air vents, (each side at the top of the windscreen).

It goes without saying that we don't do our pre-flight puffing a lighted cigarette.

Next check that the First Aid kit is in the aeroplane — usually in the pocket behind one of the seats.

Check that spare fuses are clipped inside the locker. Learn how to change a fuse quickly. On this aeroplane, depress the cartridge and twist it anti-clockwise, replace the correct amp fuse, and secure the cartridge clockwise. A little bit of cockpit time on the ground while you are waiting for your instructor one day could save delay and flapping about if ever your radio blows a fuse when you are in the air.

Check condition of starboard fuselage

Tailplane
Check general condition, and security of elevators and rudder. Check linkage and bolts and security of trim tab hinge on starboard elevator. Check condition of white navigation light on tail and make sure that the radio aerial is pointing in a straight line for maximum reception.

Underside of fuselage
Bend down and look along whole of fuselage. The amount of dirt and oil scum should not be excessive. Don't knock yourself unconscious as you straighten up.

Check port wing
Same as for starboard, but also make sure the fuel vent is clear and that the landing lights are in good condition. You have already checked the pitot tube. The small metal flap on the leading edge of the wing is the stall warner.

Check port undercarriage
As for starboard.

That's it then. Get into the aeroplane and adjust your seat. Disentangle your bit of seat belt or harness from your instructor's and tie yourself in. Remember to retract those flaps before taxying, as loose stones thrown up could damage them.

4 Starting up, and setting the altimeter

Your instructor will go through the starting up procedure with you and will probably give you a check list. The thing to avoid when using this is 'saying the words', without actually looking at the item and checking it. If you have a few minutes to yourself in the aeroplane, go through every item on the list and look at every knob and switch on the panel. Look above your head too. The air temperature gauge is usually positioned adjacent to the top of the windscreen. This gives you the outside air temperature in degrees Fahrenheit and Centigrade. The indication will always be a few degrees warmer than the actual outside temperature, so if you are flying along with a reading of a couple of degrees above freezing, be aware that icing conditions could exist. Ask your instructor to explain anything that you are not clear about.

On the Cessna 150, you will find the electrically operated flap indicator to the left above your head. This will show you the number of degrees of flap extension – four positions, 10°, 20°, 30° and 40°. On aeroplanes with manually operated flaps you will be able to hear the 'clicks' as you lower them into each position. Look outside when you are on the ground and you will get an idea of the approximate position of the flap for the amount of movement of the flap control.

Here is a typical check list for starting the aeroplane, but you should use the one provided by your instructor and go through the items in the sequence that he recommends. As you will be taking the test at your flying club, it is common sense to follow their procedures.

Fuel – ON
If you start the engine on what is left in the carburettor, it will become very quiet in a couple of minutes.

Prime – As necessary
On the first flight of the day, or if the aeroplane has been standing for some time, you will probably find it necessary to operate the primer for two or three strokes, injecting fuel directly into the float chamber to make it easier for starting. Pull the primer fully out, pause a second, then push it fully in, then repeat. Lock primer knob into slot.

Mixture – RICH
The mixture control knob is usually red. Make sure that this is pushed fully in, (the rich position).

Below 5,000 feet, the mixture should remain rich. When you are outside the hanger at the end of your flight, you will be shown how to lean the mixture to stop the engine, by pulling the knob out towards you.

You are now checking that it is rich for starting, because the previous student may have forgotten to push the knob back in after shut down, ready for the next person.

If you fly above 5,000 feet, where the air is thinner, you will be shown how to lean the mixture to achieve the correct ratio of air to fuel for most efficient operation. Unless you are flying in mountainous areas, it is unlikely that during your training you will be above 5,000 feet for extended periods, so keep the mixture rich.

Throttle
Check for full and free movement, and set approximately $\frac{1}{4}$ inch (pushing the knob away from you towards the instrument panel).

Carburettor Heat – Cold
The knob should be in, flush with the panel.

Master Switch – ON

Magnetos – ON BOTH

Brakes – ON
If you have an efficient hand brake on your aeroplane, by all means use it, but keep your feet on the brakes as a safety precaution.

Check – ALL CLEAR

Before starting the engine, have a very good look all round the aeroplane, (from where you are sitting, of course), and it is recommended that you open your side window and shout, 'CLEAR', before operating the starter. Generally, at a flying school, everyone is treating the propeller area with healthy respect, but one day you might take the aeroplane off to an Air Show, and a good warning shout will alert any wandering child to move away from the propeller.

Starter – Operate

There is usually a knob to pull or a button to push. Have your right hand on the throttle when you are starting, and once the engine is running, set the rpm at approximately 1,000.

Oil Pressure – Check

Look at the gauge to make sure that the indicator is coming up into the 'green'. If there is no movement after about thirty seconds, close the engine down and tell the engineer.

Radio – Switch On

Give it a chance to warm up before calling the Tower for taxy clearance. In the early stages your instructor will be handling the radio.

The controller will give him the runway in use and the altimeter pressure settings in millibars, (the QNH and the QFE). These are relics of a code used many years ago, known as the 'Q' code. Only a few are still in use, and these two are particularly important. When you set the QNH on the small scale of the altimeter, you will read your altitude above Mean Sea Level. With the QFE set, the reading will be height above the reference datum of the airfield, which is usually the Apron. If you have difficulty remembering which is which, perhaps it will help if you think of the N in the QNH as standing for nautical (sea level) and the F in the QFE as standing for field (airfield).

If you are flying from an airfield which is 100 feet above sea level, with the QNH set in the window, the altimeter should read 100 feet. (Airfield elevations are shown on your map and in the Air Pilot.) If the QFE is set your height should read 0 feet, for you are on the ground. The altimeter works rather like an aneroid barometer, being affected by changing pressures as your aeroplane climbs from dense air near the ground to thinner air higher up. Pressure is fed into the instrument case from the static vent, remember.

Suppose we are given a QNH of 1017, and when we set this on the altimeter, instead of reading 100 feet, we read 160 feet.

From this we would know that the altimeter itself is slightly inaccurate, so we alter it to read 100 feet, which we know is our altitude above Mean Sea Level. We then find we have a reading on the scale of 1015, (2 millibars less than the correct setting given to us by the Tower). We leave this set, but must remember to subtract 2 millibars from any pressures that we are given when we are flying before setting them on the altimeter. Each millibar is approximately 30 feet, so that accounts for the 60 feet too high that we were showing. Of course, the same thing applies if our altimeter is under-reading, and we would then add the number of millibars to any future settings given.

If we were going into the circuit for an hour, we would want to have the QFE set, giving us 0 height on landing, so we must notice if the setting they give us puts us 50 feet underground — your landings won't carve that much of a furrow.

5 Taxying, and pre-take off checks

Landing into wind

If you don't already have a plan of the runways and taxyways at your airport, try to get one as soon as possible, or make a rough sketch yourself. Some airport layouts are quite confusing, so the sooner you become familiar with yours, the better. Meanwhile, your instructor will guide you to the correct runway.

Take a good look all round, then release the handbrake by depressing the foot brakes. You will hear a click as they are disengaged. Now slightly increase the power to overcome the inertia of the aeroplane from the standstill position and roll forward a few feet. Close the throttle and gently apply the brakes to make sure they work – it is easier to get them fixed outside the hanger than to find out on landing, as you continue to roll, gulping, towards the fence.

Moving forward now, control your direction with the rudder pedals and ease back on the throttle, as necessary, to keep your speed fairly slow, rather than using the brakes. Try to stay in the centre of the taxyway. (Look in your aviation law book to see who has the right-of-way when approaching or overtaking, both in the air and on the ground. It's a certain bet you'll have a question on this in your examination, and you'll need to know for your own benefit too.) Your instructor will show you the correct speed for taxying – the important thing is always to have control of your aeroplane,

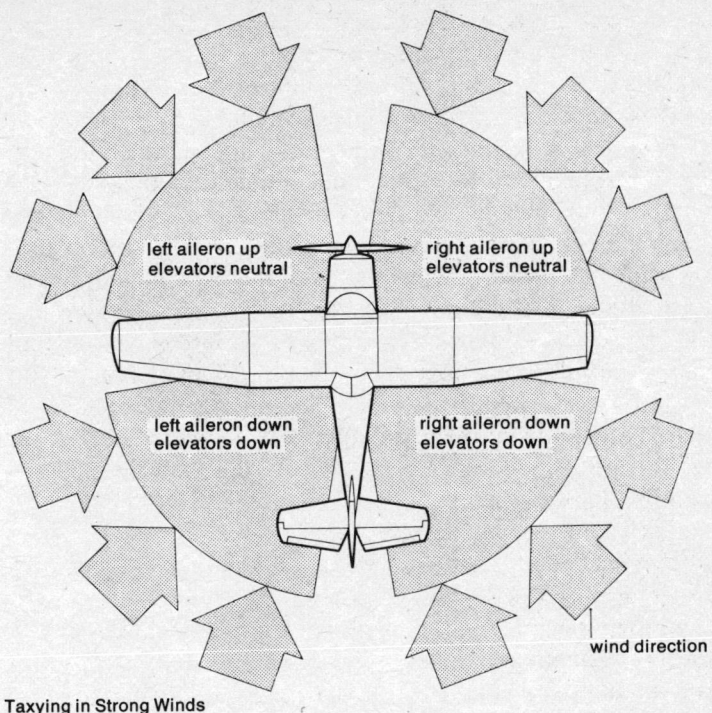

left aileron up
elevators neutral

right aileron up
elevators neutral

left aileron down
elevators down

right aileron down
elevators down

wind direction

Taxying in Strong Winds

and to be especially cautious when taxying close to other aircraft, buildings and people. Those wings are wide and that propeller lethal.

Avoid taxying through large puddles of water, so that you keep the brakes dry, or through loose stones and grit, which could damage the propeller tips.

Steering with the control column as if you are driving a car won't turn the aeroplane on the ground, but you may find yourself doing it the first few times – most students do this until they get used to guiding with their feet. However, do keep one hand on the control column as a matter of habit. Perhaps one day it will be gusty and you will need to have control of the ailerons. Keep your right hand on the throttle.

As you turn corners, you will need to ease back on the throttle a fraction, using rudder in the direction of turn and also, possibly, a little brake on the same side.

It might be necessary for you to enter or cross another runway on the way to the 'holding point', so be prepared to slow down, and if necessary stop, as you approach these intersections. Even when you have received clearance from the Tower to cross, keep a good lookout yourself, for it is always possible that someone may be using the runway unknown to the controller.

You will be shown how to place the controls as you taxy across, or downwind. If the wind is blowing between the nose and the starboard wing, move the control column to the right, so that the starboard aileron is raised, and keep the elevators neutral. If it is between the starboard wing and the tail, move the control column forward and to the left, so that the right aileron is lowered and the elevators are down. With the wind from the left, move the controls in the opposite direction. If the wind is blowing on your tail, keep the ailerons neutral and push the control column forward, so that the elevators are down. The wind against the lowered elevators will help to stop your tail from rising. The same placement of the controls should be used if you are taxying close to other aeroplanes, as the slipstream from their propellers has the same effect as the wind, but always allow plenty of spacing between yourself and the 'big boys'.

After your first few lessons, when you are thoroughly used to taxying, your instructor will show you how to check the instruments.

Allowing a few minutes after starting the engine for your directional gyro to reach its proper rotor speed, you can set this to the reading shown on the magnetic compass before starting to taxy. You will then be able to see how much it has 'precessed' from the heading set by the time you reach the holding point. To set the gyro, pull out the knob at the bottom of the instrument case and turn it until the numbers are the same as those on the magnetic compass. Be careful to double check for accuracy. For instance, it is easy to set 300° instead of 030°, because of the way the figures are presented. Now push the knob back in, and give it a turn to make sure the card doesn't continue to rotate. Remember to re-set the directional gyro before take-off, and have another quick look at it when you are lined up in the centre of the runway – it should read the same as the runway direction.

Runways are aligned by reference to Magnetic North, using the 360° in the compass. Only the first two figures are used, so if your runway is pointing to the West (270°), it would be known as 27. 030° would be known as runway 03, and so on. There are a few things to know about the magnetic compass, which you will find in your books.

When you are making a left turn during taxying, you will see that the turn needle moves to the left, and the ball skids to the right. This is correct, just as in a right turn on the ground, the needle moves to the right and the ball to the left. On a turn co-ordinator, the 'needle' is in the form of a small aeroplane, so the wing will dip to the left or right as the case may be. Don't get confused with the artificial horizon, (also indicated with a small aeroplane), which once erected, should remain steady while taxying. The turn co-ordinator is the one with the ball in the semicircular tube at the bottom of the instrument case, and the aeroplane (or needle) above it. These are actually two different instruments in one case.

While making a left turn you check that the numbers on your directional gyro and magnetic compass are decreasing; in a right turn they should be increasing. If you only have a short way to taxy before reaching the holding point you will have to make the most of the turning space available, but with some way to go, chances are you will be turning to the left and right anyway.

As you come up towards the holding point, which is about fifty feet short of the runway, your instructor will show you how to move the aeroplane over to the left side of the taxyway, so that others can get by if necessary, and how to turn into wind to allow maximum cooling for the engine while you do your power checks prior to take off.

You will normally be able to see the wind sock from your position. The wind blows through the sock from the large to the small end, so if you line up with the nose of the aeroplane pointing from the small end towards the large opening, you will be into wind. Where no wind sock is visible, turn the aeroplane, still on the left side of the taxyway, so that it is parallel to the take off runway, pointing in the direction of take off. Aeroplanes always take off and land 'into wind', or as nearly so as possible.

Follow on your check list as you go through the take off checks with your instructor. With your feet firmly on the brakes, smoothly open up the throttle to 1,700 rpm. Now check the magnetos, by turning the switch (or key) from Both to Right, note the drop in rpm, then back to Both, allowing time for the rpm to rise again, then to Left, noting the drop, before coming back to Both again. You are checking for a maximum allowable drop in each magneto, (120 rpm), and also for a maximum allowable difference between the drop in each magneto, (75 rpm). The right magneto switch is to the left side of the switch positions when looked at from your seat.

Still with 1,700 rpm set, check the carburettor heat control. Pull out the knob and notice the small drop in rpm as heated, thinner air enters the carburettor, then return the knob to 'Cold' again.

Now check the ammeter for positive charge, and the suction gauge for sufficient suction, (3 to 5 inches), to allow proper operation of your gyro instruments, (except the turn needle, which has an electrically operated gyro). Check the oil pressure and oil temperature gauges to make sure they are indicating 'in the green'. Sometimes on a very cold day it takes a while before the oil temperature registers, but the oil pressure must be there, as we said back at the starting point.

You will now do a 'slow running' check by closing the throttle completely to make sure the engine still keeps going at a low rpm, then easing the power back to 1,000 rpm.

Next, set the trim to neutral, tighten the throttle friction nut sufficiently for ease of operation, double check that the mixture is rich, that the magnetos are on 'Both', and that you have sufficient fuel for the flight. Flaps are not normally used for take-off in a light aeroplane, for although they increase the lift, the rate of climb is not so good because of the extra drag they cause. Check the directional gyro again and re-set it if necessary. Make sure that the cabin doors are locked and that your harness, (and your instructor's) is secure — you don't want him to escape yet.

Lastly, check the controls for full and free movement. Try not to make the common mistake of moving the control column to the left and right without checking to see that the ailerons are moving in the correct sense. Move the control column to the left and look out to see that the left aileron is up and the right one is down. Move the control column to the right and check that the right one is up and the left one is down. It has been known for aeroplanes to come from a maintenance check improperly rigged, and now is the time to find out.

Once you are satisfied that you have checked your aeroplane properly, turn around to face the runway before telling the Tower that you are ready for take-off. There are two reasons for turning before calling. One is that you will be able to see other aeroplanes approaching on 'finals' to land, (landing aircraft have priority), and the other is that if the controller clears you for an 'immediate take-off', you will already be in a position to taxy straight on to the runway without wasting valuable time turning from your 'into wind' position. Chances are that if you have been given clearance for an immediate take-off, he is trying to slot you in before another one lands.

Some of the points covered in the last few chapters will be learned gradually during the whole of your training. As with anything new, there seems a lot to learn, but you are obviously not expected to know everything at once. If you can fasten on to one or two background points each time you fly, you will be doing well.

6 Effects of controls

Purple Airways are for Royal Flights

From now on, before you fly, your instructor will give you a quick briefing on the various things that will be covered in the air. He will probably use a small model aeroplane to illustrate the points he is making. This morning you will be going through the effects of the various controls – the ailerons, (at the back of the wings), the elevators, (horizontal at the end of the tailplane), and the rudder, (mounted vertically at the back of the fin). Another very important item to be covered is the use of the trim.

On the pre-flight inspection, we looked at the elevator trim tab, which is hinged at the back of the starboard elevator. This is operated by a wheel in the cockpit, to the right of your seat. When you wind the wheel forward, (down, away from you), the trim tab on the elevator is actually moving up, in the opposite direction to the way you are winding. When you wind the wheel back, the trim tab outside is moving down. Prove this to yourself when you go out to the aeroplane. We will come on to the use of the trim once we are in the air, for we are going to take each of the items and go through them as if we were sitting in the aeroplane. We will also jot down a few 'pre-flight' reminders where necessary.

Here we are in our Cessna 150, clear of controlled airspace, on a nice sunny day. Just take a look at the position of the aeroplane's nose in relation to the outside horizon.

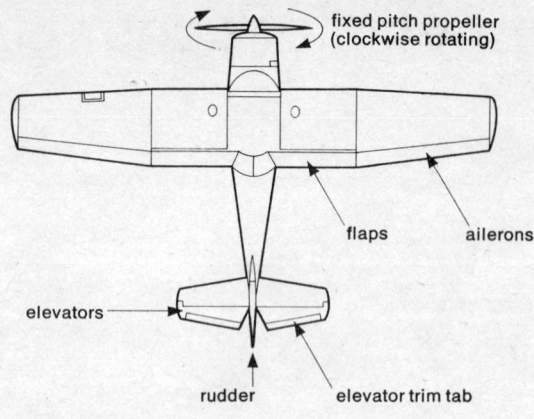

fixed pitch propeller
(clockwise rotating)

flaps

ailerons

elevators

rudder

elevator trim tab

Cessna 150

We'll start with the elevators. If we push the control column forward, away from us, you'll see that the nose goes down below the horizon, and if we now move the control column back towards us, the nose will rise above the horizon. Notice that our airspeed increases as we lower the nose, and decreases as we raise the nose.

(*Pre-flight:* As we move the control column forward, the elevators are moved down. The airflow against the down elevators forces the tail up, making the nose of the aeroplane move down. If we move the control column back, the elevators are moved up, the airflow over the raised elevators forces the tail down, so that the aircraft nose comes up).

Now let's look at the ailerons. If we move the control column to the left, you'll see that the left wing goes down below the horizon and the right wing comes up above it. If we now move the control column to the right, the right wing moves down and the left wing comes up.

(*Pre-flight:* Taking the first case, the left aileron will move up and the right one down. The right wing will now have more lifting action than the left wing, as we have slightly increased its top surface area, and this is what starts the initial roll or bank to the left. Pressure is lower on the top of the wing than underneath it, and it is the low pressure that produces most of the lift while flying).

Coming on to the rudder next, let's put the nose of the aeroplane on that clump of trees on the horizon. If we push the left rudder pedal forward, you will see the nose move to the left, away from our point, and if we move the right rudder pedal, the nose will yaw to the right, back to the trees.

(*Pre-flight:* As we move the left rudder pedal, the rudder will move to the left and the airflow against its surface will push the tail round to the right, yawing the nose of the aeroplane to the left. With the right rudder pedal depressed, the rudder moves to the right, the airflow moves the tail to the left and the nose yaws to the right).

Let's just look at each of the controls again. If we move the control column and rudder pedals slowly, the result or effect will be slow, and if we move them quickly, the effect on the control surfaces will be more rapid. Also, we find that by moving the controls a small amount, we achieve a small effect, and that a large movement will give us a large effect. Incidentally, we don't ever want to use any of the controls harshly – a gentle touch is the aim.

We'll now put the aeroplane into a banked attitude, so that the horizon is no longer horizontal to the wings. Going through each of the controls again, we find that they work in exactly the same way as they did before, and the only thing that has changed is the outside reference.

Having had a look at the primary effects of the controls, we'll now go on to the further or secondary effects, using just one control at a time.

With the elevators we find that there are no further effects. We push the control column down and the nose goes down. We pull it up and the nose comes up.

Now we'll have another look at the ailerons. Remember, we are not using the elevators or the rudder this time. We know that if we move the control column to the left, the left wing moves down and the right wing moves up. If we keep the control column over to the left for a few moments, we find that the bank starts to increase, and if you watch the nose of the aeroplane you will see that it yaws to the left, dipping below the horizon, even though we are not using any rudder. We are now in a descending spiral to the left, with our airspeed increasing.
(*Pre-flight:* Once the bank has started, the aeroplane will sideslip towards the low wing. The high wing – in this case the right wing – is getting more lift from the extra airflow over it, and this increases the bank. The airflow meeting the left side of the fuselage weathercocks the tail round to the right, yawing the nose of the aeroplane to the left, and since we are in a banked attitude, the nose will move below the horizon).

Let's now use the rudder on its own. We know that if we apply right rudder we yaw to the right. By holding on the right rudder, in a few moments the left wing will start to come up, the bank will increase, the nose will drop below the horizon, and we will enter a spiral descent to the right.
(*Pre-flight:* As the nose yaws to the right, the aeroplane will tend to skid in its original direction due to inertia, resulting in the inner, (right), wing being somewhat shielded from the

airflow by the fuselage. This is one reason that the left wing is getting more lift than the right wing. It also gets more lift, hence the bank, because it is travelling faster, being on the outside of the turn).

The whole point of showing you these further effects is to emphasise the importance of using all the controls in co-ordination. This spiral descent that develops is not the same as a 'spin', which you may have heard about, and which will be covered in a later lesson. One of the differences, since we have mentioned it, is that we have an increasingly high airspeed in the spiral descent, and a constant low airspeed in the spin.

Let's move on to the effects of the airspeed. If we lower the nose we know our airspeed is going to increase, and if we now move all the controls – the ailerons, the elevators, and the rudder – we find we have a firm, effective reaction because of the resistance to the airflow. If we now raise the nose, the airspeed decreases and when we try out the controls again we notice considerably less 'feel': we have to move the control column and rudder pedals more to get an effective result. Notice that with a fixed pitch propeller the rpm increases with an increase in airspeed and decreases as we raise the nose and reduce the airspeed. Most training aeroplanes have the propeller fixed at one pitch angle.

On to the next thing. We'll keep the airspeed at 70 miles an hour and increase the throttle setting so that we can try the controls with a strong slipstream from the propeller. Then, still keeping the same airspeed, we'll reduce the slipstream by closing the throttle. We now find that the elevators and rudder are less effective, although the ailerons feel much the same.

(*Pre-flight:* The slipstream from the propeller is thrown back along the fuselage and over the tail section which houses the elevators and rudder, but as the ailerons are on the outside of the wings they are not affected by the increase or decrease in the slipstream).

Now the trim. If we lower the nose you'll feel that you are holding forward, or down pressure on the control column. If you wind the trimming wheel forward, or down away from you, this pressure will be relieved. Relax that grip – you'll be able to feel it better. If you now pull back on the control column you'll feel the weight that you are holding up, so wind the trimming wheel back up towards you until the pressure goes. Practise this a bit. The important thing is to put the aeroplane where you want it with the elevators and then trim off the pressure. Each time you think you have it about right, take your hand off the control column and see if the aeroplane starts to climb or descend. If it does, correct the attitude with the elevators and then re-trim.

(*Pre-flight:* Once you have mastered accurate trimming, a lot of the work will be taken out of your flying and on cross country flights you will only have to make minor adjustments while you concentrate on map reading.

You may be a little confused about the trim tab. Remember that with the control column forward, the elevators will be down and the airflow beneath them forces the tail up moving the nose down. As you are holding forward pressure on the control column, you wind the trim wheel in the cockpit forward. The trim tab on the starboard elevator moves up so that a certain amount of airflow strikes the tab and holds the elevators down for you.

If you pull back on the control column, the elevators move up and the airflow against them forces the tail down, moving the nose up. You wind the trim wheel beside you back, the trim tab moves down and the airflow against the tab holds the elevators up for you. Think about it –

Not much more to cover in this lesson now. Let's move on to what happens when we increase and decrease power with the throttle. We'll find another reference point on the horizon – that brown field will do. As we increase power by pushing the throttle in, you will see the nose rise above the horizon and also yaw to the left away from the field. When we decrease power the nose will drop and yaw to the right. Notice that the rpm increases as we increase the throttle setting and decreases when we reduce the power.

(*Pre-flight:* The slipstream is deflected back, corkscrewing round the fuselage. With a clockwise rotating propeller, as we add power this helical slipstream strikes the left side of the fuselage and yaws the nose to the left rather like a weather-vane. Also, with an increase in power there will be an increased downwash of air on the tailplane, forcing the nose up. With a reduction in power, the rotating propeller will overcome the slipstream effect, yawing the nose to the right, and the reduced slipstream will allow the nose to drop. With an anti-clockwise rotating propeller the yaw will be in the reverse direction, but just concentrate on the one you are flying – one is all any of us can handle at a time, just so long as it keeps rotating.

On to the flaps now. First, look at the position of the nose on the horizon again, and also note our airspeed. Always be careful not to lower the flaps if this is above the flap limiting speed – 100 mph on this aeroplane – as they could be overstressed if they are suddenly dumped into a fast airflow. If necessary we must reduce the power and wait a moment until the airspeed decreases. As the flaps are lowered, you will see the nose of the aeroplane 'balloon' up, and we also have a reduction in airspeed. As we raise them, notice that we sink and the airspeed picks up again. One day you might be coming in to land and decide to overshoot and go round again, but you must be careful not to raise the flaps below 200 feet, and then bring them up 10° at a time, so that you can control the necessary trim changes more easily. Let's just have another look at that sink. Watch the altimeter and see how much height we lose by bringing the flaps up all at once. That height loss would have been unpleasant close to the ground. (*Pre-flight:* The purpose of the flaps is to increase the lift by extending the wing area, enabling us to fly safely at a slower airspeed. As well as the extra lift we have the disadvantage of extra drag, due to the flaps extending into the airstream, and if we want to maintain our original airspeed, we have to lower the nose, which also gives us a good view ahead of the aeroplane for landing).

Two last items before you doze off. We've already mentioned the mixture control. Just remember to keep the knob in the rich position, (flush with the panel), below 5,000 feet.

The carburettor heat control is fully in when cold, and fully out when heat is applied. Some aeroplanes, such as the Cessna 150, have engines which are susceptible to carburettor icing in conditions of high relative humidity, and during long descents with the engine idling. We apply carburettor heat before closing the throttle to be on the safe side.

Next time you will be starting to apply some of the things you have learned today, with your instructor breathing down your neck to jog your memory.

7 Straight and level

Today you will learn to fly the aeroplane in a straight direction at a constant level altitude – not as easy as it sounds and it takes quite a lot of practice.

Before starting we'll have a good look out, as it's no fun if we maintain our level and direction and fly straight into somebody else. If you spot another aeroplane just tell me its 'clock position' – you can tell the time, can't you?

We'll fly at an altitude of 2,000 feet, using a power setting of 2,300 rpm. Taking the level first, we adjust the attitude of the nose with the elevators and then trim off the pressure. Glance back at the altimeter and you'll see we have slipped to 1,900 feet, so raise the nose again and just before the needle gets to 2,000 feet, ease the control column forward – a very small amount, as we are only talking about 100 feet. Now look out to see if the nose is in approximately the same position as before. Hold this attitude and now re-trim.

In turbulent conditions it will be more difficult to hold an exact altitude. We might have lost that 100 feet because you were unaware of holding a slight pressure on the control column, or perhaps we were incorrectly trimmed. Once the trim is right, even if we let go, the aeroplane will return to its original attitude, so take your hands off the control column and see what happens to the nose. What happens to your instructor is something else.

Let's now fly towards that lake on the horizon – notice

where it is on the windscreen. Keep your wings level with the ailerons. Each wing tip should be the same distance from the horizon. Later on you will be using the directional gyro to keep straight, but for the moment, concentrate on looking outside at your point, glancing at the altimeter to check your altitude, and watching for other traffic.

Note that with an rpm setting of 2,300, we have an indicated airspeed of 95 miles per hour. The inner ring on the airspeed indicator is in knots (nautical miles).

I'll just show you that it is possible to maintain our altitude and fly towards our lake by lowering one wing and using opposite rudder to keep straight. However, this isn't a practical way to fly – it feels awkward and the extra drag of the banked wing causes a reduction in airspeed. It is fairly obvious to us when we are flying along with a wing down like this, but there are times when you might not notice that one of the wings is slightly low. This is when we can use the slip indicator – the ball in the curved glass tube.

If you see that the ball has moved outside those lines in the centre of the tube, it could mean that you are unconsciously holding a little rudder to counteract a low wing and keep the nose on the reference point. If the ball has moved to the right, use a little right rudder to bring it back to the centre. If it has moved to the left, use left rudder. You will hear the expression, 'eliminate yaw', and this is what we are doing. Think of it as 'stepping on the ball' with the appropriate foot. Just slight pressure though – don't put the boot in.

Now look at the wings and level them up equally each side with the horizon. While this is going on you will probably find that you are no longer headed towards your point. If you have moved to the left, use a little right aileron and a touch of right rudder to bring the nose back again. Glance back at the altimeter and have another good look outside – there's a Concorde up there at 3 o'clock, but we'll never catch it now.

On to the next thing. If we increase our power we know that the nose will rise – remember? So as we open up the throttle we will have to ease forward on the control column in order to stay at 2,000 feet. We also know that the nose will yaw to the left as we increase power. If we allow this to happen we will move away from our point, so we must be ready with a little right rudder to keep straight.

Now, increase the power to 2,400 rpm, apply slight forward pressure and enough right rudder to keep that ball in the centre. You are holding forward pressure so need to trim slightly forward. Perhaps one day you will need to increase your airspeed in order to reach an airfield before dark, but you will also need to maintain your altitude and direction.

If we reduce the power to 2,200 rpm, do you remember what will happen to the nose? Correct, it will drop, and it will also yaw to the right. Therefore, as we decrease power we need to hold slight back pressure on the control column to maintain 2,000 feet, and to apply a touch of left rudder to keep straight. As we are holding the aeroplane up, we wind the trim wheel up to take the weight off the control column. The nose is now higher in relation to the horizon and our airspeed is lower than before. Perhaps one day Air Traffic Control will ask you to reduce your airspeed when they are trying to slot you in with other landing traffic.

You are not alone if you are bewildered about the yaw and which rudder to use. You are actually applying rudder in the opposite direction to the way the nose yaws. Normally, there is no need to hold constant rudder because corrections are built into the aeroplane.

If we continue to decrease the power, we have to hold the nose up further each time, to stay at 2,000 feet, increasing the angle of attack of the wings to the relative airflow to give us more lift. As we do this, our airspeed continues to decrease until eventually the power we have is not sufficient to overcome the extra drag and we have to lower the nose and lose height, or increase the power to keep height.

To fly slowly with the flaps down – first remembering to check the flap limiting speed – we will have to use extra power to stay at the same altitude and lower the nose slightly to give us a safe airspeed. This extra power will give us more effect from the elevators and rudder, remember, and will counteract the increased drag of the flaps.

We have found that a power setting of 2,300 rpm gives us an airspeed of 95 miles an hour, so if we decide to fly at 100 mph, we know we will have to increase the rpm, but we won't know by how much. Let's try increasing it to 2,450 rpm, remembering to ease the nose forward and eliminate the yaw. Allow the airspeed to settle. This gives us 115 mph, so we'll ease back to 2,400 rpm. We check that and keep making small adjustments until we are flying at exactly the required 110 mph, and then we trim.

The same goes for a lower airspeed. If we want 80 miles per hour, we will need less than 2,300 rpm, so let's try 2,100 rpm, easing back on the control column, keeping the ball in the centre. We find this only gives us 75 mph, so we increase the rpm slightly. Remember to allow time for the airspeed to settle each time – a few moments – before making further adjustments. Now check that you are still flying towards your reference point, maintain your altitude, and look out.

If you can master flying straight and level, with accurate trimming, you have really achieved something.

8 Climbing

We'll just run through a few points before we start today. As always, we must maintain a good lookout for other aeroplanes, especially up ahead. With a high nose attitude, we won't be able to see immediately underneath the aeroplane, so every five hundred feet we will move the nose to one side, clear ourselves below, and then continue on our original climb path.

Because the aircraft nose will block our view of the horizon, we can choose a cloud as a reference point for keeping straight. They do move, but not fast enough to prevent us pinpointing one for a few minutes' climb. On the rare occasion when there is no cloud, pick yourself a point to the left of the nose and try not to creep into it or away from it while you are climbing. If you have a good straight road or railway on your left, you can use that.

We have to keep an eye on our engine oil pressure and temperature – remember, we want to keep them 'in the green'. We will be climbing with a power setting of 2,500 rpm and maintaining an airspeed of 70 miles an hour, so with this high power setting, low airspeed and high nose attitude, the engine won't get as much cooling from the airflow as in level flight. If we notice that the temperature is starting to come up, we'll level off and allow the engine to cool for a few minutes before continuing with the climb.

We can use a good memory aid to help us with the sequence

for entering the climb – PAT (Power, Attitude, Trim). First increase the power to 2,500 rpm. You will feel, and see, the nose rising, which this time we allow as we want to gain height. Use a touch of right rudder to eliminate the yaw, just as you did in Straight and Level when you increased power.

Next we have our A for Attitude, so we ease back slightly on the control column and establish the climb at 70 mph. Take a look outside at the angle of the wings to the horizon and try to remember this attitude. If you keep the wings the same distance above the horizon each side, and the ball in the centre of the tube, you will be climbing in a straight line.

Lastly, we have T for Trim, so we trim off this back pressure we are holding. Glance back at the airspeed to see if we still have 70 mph. If it is a little low, move the control column forward a fraction, hold that attitude while you give the airspeed time to settle, then trim very slightly forward. If the airspeed is too high, ease back on the control column, once again giving the airspeed a chance to settle before making any further adjustments, and then trim, this time slightly back.

Our altimeter needle is moving steadily clockwise round the dial, and if you look down at the vertical speed indicator, you will see that for this power setting and airspeed, we are climbing at a rate of 450 feet per minute.

We'll now check the temperature and pressure and have another good look out. We need to see in the blind spot beneath the nose, so use right aileron and right rudder to move the nose to the right, check all clear below, then back to our climb path with left aileron and left rudder – just enough rudder to keep the ball centred.

To level off from the climb, we have a slightly different mnemonic. This time it is APT, (Attitude, Power, Trim). 'PAT is APT to climb' might help you remember which is for the climb and which for the level off. We want to stop the climb at 3,000 feet, so about 50 feet before the needle gets there, we move the control column forward to the level attitude. This will put the nose slightly higher on the horizon than the other day when we were at 2,000 feet, but you will soon learn to judge the amount of forward movement by cross-referring to the altimeter. You are now holding quite a lot of forward pressure, as you still have a high power setting.

The next step is P, so reduce the power to 2,300 rpm, (your normal straight and level setting), remembering a touch of left rudder as you come back on the throttle.

We finally come to the last part of our APT, the T for Trim, so wind the wheel forward until the forward pressure you are holding on the control column is relieved. Don't avoid the trim because you are not sure which way to wind the wheel – with practice it will become automatic. We are now flying straight and level at 3,000 feet.

Let's just take a look at climbing with the flaps down. We'll pretend we have just overshot the runway after a poor approach to land.

As we go through the same climb sequence, notice that we have a slightly lower airspeed for the same attitude, due to the increased drag from the flaps. We need to keep our airspeed at 70 miles an hour, so we have to lower the nose a fraction, which gives us a lower rate of climb, as you can see on the vertical speed indicator.

We want to gain altitude as soon as possible after overshooting and this is where the temptation comes to raise the flaps quickly, but it must be resisted You learned the other day not to bring them up below 200 feet, because of sinking back. Once we have a safe height above the ground, we raise them 10° at a time so that we can control the changing attitude. Just a point here, which will come up when you are actually overshooting at the airfield – we will always use full power then, not the 2,500 rpm we use for the normal climb.

You may find you are taught climbing and descending in one lesson, for you have climbed up and may as well use the going down to your benefit. It is quite a lot to absorb in one lesson if you combine the two, (even though you are an exceptional student), so don't let yourself become confused by trying to do too much at once. Chances are that you will have another lesson on both climbing and descending and your instructor certainly won't be pushing you before he is happy, or at least optimistic.

9 Descending

'What goes up must come down', so we'll cover descending this afternoon. In our look out, we need to include the area below, so every 500 feet we'll turn the aeroplane to clear ourselves underneath the nose, just as we did in climbing. At the same time we'll open up half throttle for a few seconds to prevent the plugs oiling up during a long glide, and also check our temperature and pressure. We will be descending at 70 miles per hour.

With climbing, we had our mnemonic of PAT to help us remember the sequence of getting into the climb, and APT for levelling off. With descending, all we have to remember is PAT for both the entry and for levelling off. (PAT, PAT down the stairs, if it helps). Right, let's pick a reference point on the horizon, and take a good look out all around.

Before closing the throttle we must remember to apply full carburettor heat, so pull the knob out towards you. Now, 'P' for Power, so close the throttle – remember a touch of left rudder to prevent the nose yawing to the right. Next, 'A' for Attitude – Hold the nose of the aeroplane level with the horizon while the airspeed decreases towards 70 mph. Make small adjustments with the elevators to get exactly 70 mph, holding each change of attitude until the airspeed has settled. Finally we come to the 'T' for Trim, so wind the wheel up until the pressure is taken off the control column. You will need to wind it back quite a large amount. It may seem strange to trim in this direction when we are going down, but remember, we started by holding the nose up level, so in effect we are holding the aeroplane up, and need to trim up to relieve the weight.

Just note our rate of descent on the vertical speed indicator. As we come down now towards 2,500 feet, smoothly apply half throttle, then close it again, check the temperature and pressure gauges, and now clear yourself below by moving the aeroplane to one side with right aileron and a little right rudder, then back to your descent path with left aileron and left rudder. You're working well.

About 50 feet before we get to 1,500 feet, open up the throttle to our cruise rpm of 2,300, ('P' for Power), and push the carburettor heat knob back to cold. Don't forget the yaw as you apply power – remember which foot to use? You will feel the nose pitching up, so apply forward pressure to stop the aeroplane climbing and check that you are flying straight and level at 1,500 feet, ('A' for Attitude). Lastly we have 'T' for Trim, so think which way you have to wind the wheel – that's right, you are applying forward pressure, so wind the wheel forward.

When you are ready, climb back to 3,000 feet and level off. We'll now take a look at descending using a power setting of 1,500 rpm, which you will use for your normal approaches at the airfield. The advantage of using power in the descent is a better response from the elevators and rudder at slower speeds – remember the 'slipstream' effect we looked at in your earlier lesson? – and you will also have a slower 'stalling speed', which is something we will come on to a couple of lessons from today. We have just been practising glide descents because there will certainly be times when you need to handle the aeroplane correctly on an approach to land without the use of power – 'forced landing' practice is one example – so we have to make sure you can descend safely both ways.

Now, as you start the descent, reduce the power to 1,500 rpm. Concentrate on establishing your correct descent attitude for an airspeed of 70 mph and accurate trimming, rather than focusing too much attention on getting the rpm exact at this stage. Notice that the nose is a little higher than it was with the throttle closed, when we had to ease it further forward to maintain our airspeed. If you glance at the vertical speed indicator you'll see that we also have a slightly lower rate of descent when we use power. You can now adjust the throttle to give you 1,500 rpm, check the airspeed and make sure you are correctly trimmed. Remember to make your descent checks every 500 feet, but this time there is no need to open up the throttle as we have enough power at 1,500 rpm to keep the engine warm.

We are now going to lower some flap. Depress the flap lever with your right hand, then look up at the flap indicator to the left of your head and watch the pointer moving down. When it gets to 20°, release the lever. Meanwhile, we want to maintain our airspeed – notice that it has reduced a little due to the drag from the lowered flap, so lower the nose and regain 70 mph, then re-trim, slightly forward.

Here we are set up just as we would be for an approach to land at the airfield. We need to concentrate not only on our descent checks, but must also maintain a particularly good look out, and – very important – watch our airspeed. If you find it has decreased, do something about it by lowering the nose. If it is high, raise the nose slightly. The airspeed is controlled by the elevators and the rate of descent is controlled by the power we apply. If we increase the throttle setting, the nose will start to rise, so we won't be losing height at the same rate as before and if we close the throttle, the nose will drop and we'll lose height more rapidly.

Let's level off now at 1,000 feet, which is the circuit height at most aerodromes. (Check the AGA section of the 'Air Pilot'). First, have a good look around, then power back to 2,300 rpm, a touch of right rudder to keep straight, slight forward pressure to stop the nose rising and then trim. You can have some more practice when we are on final approach, with both of us watching the Altimeter so that we don't plough into the runway.

10 Turning

This morning I'd like you to climb to 2,000 feet and then level off. Good. We'll start by making a level turn to the left, so in your lookout, pay particular attention to that side of the aeroplane. Just note our airspeed before we begin, as once we are turning it will be slightly less.

To enter the turn we use left aileron and just enough left rudder to keep the turn balanced, with the ball in the centre. As we are now in a banked attitude we are getting a little more drag, so we need a very slight amount of back pressure on the control column to maintain our altitude.

Look at the position of the nose on the horizon and you can see the correct angle of bank for a medium turn – not more than about 30°. Now that we are established in the turn, we find we can move the control column back to the right and still continue turning, with only small adjustments to keep the bank constant. (The outer wing is moving faster than the inner wing, which gives it more lift and causes an overbanking tendency, so we have to 'hold off' bank).

Let's now check our altitude. We've gained a little height, so relax that back pressure. Meanwhile, keep looking out to the left. You are still a bit high, so ease forward very slightly on the control column, keeping the bank on. Notice that because of the banked attitude, our airspeed is a little lower than when we were flying straight and level, but this is quite acceptable in a level turn.

Just before we come to that yellow mustard field on the horizon, we use right aileron and right rudder to come out of the turn, relaxing the back pressure we were holding so that we don't climb, and then continue to fly straight and level towards the field.

Try one to the right now, entering it just as you did before, but this time using right aileron and right rudder – a little more rudder than you needed in a turn to the left. The nose appears in a slightly different position when you turn this way because of the side by side seating in the cockpit, so try to remember the angle with the horizon you should expect to see for both a right and a left medium banked turn. Now, pick yourself a reference point and start taking off the bank just before you get to it, using left aileron and left rudder. Remember to relax that back pressure as you level out.

When you are leaving and approaching the airfield, you will be doing climbing and descending turns, so we'll look at these now. Climbing turns are entered in the same way, but we only use a small angle of bank – not more than about 15°. The important thing is to keep our airspeed constant, so as we enter the turn we must lower the nose slightly to counteract the drag of the banked attitude. If we increase the bank too much we will also be increasing the drag and will have to lower the nose still further to maintain 70 mph. If we do this, we will not have such a good rate of climb, (number of feet gained per minute), as with a small angle of bank. Look at the vertical speed indicator for a moment and we'll prove this. One more point – in the climbing turn the bank tends to increase, and we need to hold it off, just as we did in level turns. (The high wing in the climbing turn is meeting the airflow at a greater angle of attack than the low wing, giving it more lift and causing it to overbank).

When you are ready, try one to the left. I'd like to see you take an exaggerated look out all round – that furtive leer isn't enough. When you come to take the test, the examiner won't take your 'look out' for granted, so be very positive about it.

In the climbing turn, don't forget to check your oil temperature and pressure, just as you would in a straight climb. Nag yourself about the airspeed and try to keep the bank constant. I'd like you to come out of the turn at 3,000 feet and continue with a straight climb, so about 50 feet before we get there it will be right aileron and right rudder. As you take the bank off, ease very slightly back on the control column so that you maintain 70 mph. Remember, you had to depress the nose a little to maintain your airspeed in the turn. That's good – try one to the right now.

You may find it difficult to judge the angle of bank in

climbing turns, because your outside reference is continually changing, but it will come with practice. Your instructor may allow you to assess your angle of bank by glancing at the artificial horizon, which is graduated in 30°, 60° and 90° marks. However, he will cover it up if he sees you with your eyes glued to it. If you can get the bank correct by looking outside, you have achieved more than by using a 'crutch', so work yourself. You are paying a lot of money for this and need to get the maximum benefit.

At 4,000 feet, stop the turn and continue a straight climb to 5,000 feet, then level off.

Just refresh your memory now on descending without power. We'll begin with a straight descent, and then go into a descending turn to the left, using left aileron and left rudder. As we enter the turn, we lower the nose slightly to maintain 70 mph. Once again we'll be using a small angle of bank, because if we increased the bank, we would also increase the drag, and would have to lower the nose to keep our airspeed correct, causing a higher than normal rate of descent. This time we have to hold the bank on, because the inner wing is meeting the airflow at a greater angle of attack as we circle down, which compensates for the extra lift from the faster moving outer wing.

Continue descending to the left, not forgetting the normal 500 feet checks. At 3,000 feet, continue with a straight descent, raising the nose slightly as you come out of the turn, so that you maintain your airspeed. Now let's have one to the right.

When you are established in the turn, I'd like you to increase the power to 1,500 rpm, keeping the aeroplane turning and adjusting the attitude to maintain 70 mph. The nose will be slightly higher, remember, and the rate of descent will be less. Stop the turn at 1,500 feet and continue a straight descent to 1,000 feet, then level off and fly straight and level. Just push the carburettor heat knob back to cold.

Staying at 1,000 feet, make a level turn to the left now, then straighten up and look ahead to see if you can spot the airfield. Notice how it looks on a rather hazy day like this — there's a large hangar over to the right that shows up well and a big patch of dark trees to the left. You'll soon get used to picking out the familiar shapes of 'home'. Meanwhile, let's get back to 1,000 feet. The more you can divide your attention and still keep flying accurately, the easier it will become and the better you will be doing. Smile — you're supposed to be enjoying this.

11   Stalling

This afternoon I'd like you to follow me through on the take off, as once we have stalling and spinning out of the way, you will be starting in the circuit and doing the take offs and landings yourself, heavily monitored by Big Brother, of course. When we are airborne, we'll climb to 4,000 feet and you can do some climbing turns on the way up, just to see how much you have forgotten — such confidence I have in you.

We go through stalls simply to make sure you can recover from them promptly and correctly if you ever inadvertently get into one, especially near the ground, when it is essential to recover with a minimum loss of height.

Let's just go back to our pre-flight briefing for a moment. A stall occurs when the wings are presented to the relative airflow at too great an angle of attack, so they can happen at any airspeed and in any attitude relative to the horizon, if we ignore all the symptoms of the approaching stall.

Before we show you how easy it is to recover, we'll go through our pre-stall (HASELL) checks together:

H – *for Height*
Sufficient to recover by 3,000 feet, which we have, as we are still maintaining 4,000 feet.

A – *for Airframe*
If we had been flying with our flaps down, we would now retract them.

S – *for Security*
We'll make sure our harness is secure and tuck any loose articles in the back of the aeroplane. Let's put that map and check list down by the side of the seat, along with your worry beads.

E – *for Engine*
Check the temperature and pressure gauges, and make sure the mixture is rich. Before closing the throttle, we'll remember to apply carburettor heat, but we'll carry on with the rest of the checks first.

L – *for Location*
Check that we are out of controlled airspace and not over any airfields or built up areas.

Lastly, another **L** *for Lookout*
We'll turn the aeroplane to the left through about 90°, and then back to the right, having a very good search of the area, particularly underneath. Right, so we're all clear.

First, I'm going to show you a stall recovery without using power, and then we'll do one correctly by applying full power at the stall, so that you can compare the height we lose during the recovery. We have plenty of altitude at 4,000 feet to practise until you are thoroughly confident.

We'll now apply carburettor heat and close the throttle. As we try to maintain our altitude by continually easing back on the control column, let's pick out the symptoms of the stall. First, there goes the stall warner, which sounds about 10 miles an hour before the stall. Not all aeroplanes have one, but this one does, so we are obviously not going to ignore it. Another symptom, the controls are starting to feel slack and unresponsive. Notice the high nose attitude, and the decreasing airspeed. Now we feel a slight buffeting as the airflow breaks up over the tailplane – and there's the stall, at about 45 mph. See the nose drop? Let's check our altimeter – 4,100 feet.

We're going to recover by lowering the nose to reduce the angle of attack, and this time we won't use any power. Here we are quite quickly at flying speed again, levelling out at 3,600 feet, but just look at the amount of height we've lost. That 500 feet near the ground would be disconcerting, to say the least, so we must always use full power in the recovery.

Right, you climb the aeroplane back to 4,000 feet, and we'll compare the height loss by recovering correctly. Once again, we'll run through our HASELL checks. Now, carburettor heat, close the throttle, watch for the symptoms so that you learn to recognise them – and there's the stall at 3,900 feet.

Correct recovery – Full power, a touch of right rudder to prevent yaw, lower the nose by moving the control column straight forward sufficiently to unstall the wings, and then ease back to level flight, reducing the power to the normal cruise setting of 2,300 rpm. This time we've lost about 75 feet.

You have a go now and I'll talk you through. Just get the sequence in your mind. HASELL checks, carburettor heat, power off, try to maintain height, recognize the symptoms of the approaching stall. Once you have stalled, (sometimes it is not very definite and the aeroplane is 'mushing down', which you can tell by monitoring the altimeter), FULL power promptly, a touch of rudder, forward movement of the control column – not a very large amount – and then ease back up to the horizon, bringing the power back to 2,300 rpm. Fine. Just remember to push the carburettor heat back to cold now that the drama is over. Have one or two more goes until you are happy about it yourself.

Now let's look at a stall occurring when we have a power setting of 1,500 rpm. The recovery action is exactly the same. Notice that the airspeed falls more slowly and that the stall occurs at a lower airspeed. Also, with a 'power on' stall, there is a tendency for one of the wings to drop, but we won't know which one until we stall. The important thing to remember is first to use the **Standard correct recovery** – full power, control column straight forward, (resisting the temptation to use the ailerons, as this will only make matters worse), and then, as a secondary consideration, a little rudder opposite to the dropped wing to prevent the nose yawing further towards it. If the left wing has dropped, we use right rudder, and if it's the right wing, we use left rudder. Once we have recovered from the stall, we can level the wings with aileron and ease back to level flight. Just have a bit of practice, and then we'll go on to stalling with the flaps down.

This time when we do our HASELL checks, we'll lower the flaps when we come to A for Airframe, first making sure we are below the flap limiting speed. If you ever forget what this is, you can tell by looking at the top of the white arc on the airspeed indicator. (The bottom of the white arc is the calibrated stalling speed for this aeroplane, with the power off and flaps down. When we get back we'll take a look at all those colour markings on the airspeed indicator – remind me).

First we'll do a flaps down stall, using no power as we

enter. Notice that the speed falls quickly, and there is only a short warning before the stall. When it occurs, we have a very low indicated airspeed, and once again we have this wing drop tendency. This time the right wing has dropped.

Standard recovery action – full power, control column forward, and then a touch of left rudder to prevent further yaw towards the right wing. Now level the wings and ease out of the dive. With flaps down, we must keep an eye on our airspeed during the recovery so that we don't exceed the flap limiting speed. That time we lost 150 feet, so let's try it again and see if we can recover with no height loss at all.

Just climb back up to 4,000 feet and we'll go through the stall that might occur under approach conditions. This is simply using your approach power of 1,500 rpm, which we have already covered, combined with flaps down, which we have just done. If you ever stall on the approach, perhaps because your attention has been diverted, (shame on you), and you haven't been alerted to the impending stall by the symptoms we've just been recognising, remember to use the standard recovery procedure. Even if you are turning at the time, the control column should still be moved forward in a straight line as you apply full power.

The more quickly and efficiently you recover, the less height you will lose, and remember that if you recognise the symptoms and promptly recover, you won't get into a stall in the first place, but if you do stall, the correct recovery action will bring you out of it.

As the visibility is so good today, let's climb up to 5,000 feet and go through some spinning.

12 Spinning

On the ground we said that a spin results from yawing the aeoplane at the point of stall, so if you don't get into a stall, you won't get into a spin. We teach you how to spin and recover just to make sure you know how to get out of one correctly should the need ever arise. It's not particularly unpleasant and some people actually enjoy it, so you can forget all those horror stories.

While we are in the spin, you will see – because I'll make you open your eyes – that we have a constant low airspeed. If you think back to your first lesson when we did descending spirals, you'll remember that the airspeed was fairly high, and we were able to recover by using opposite aileron and rudder and raising the elevators. Spin recovery is different, as we'll see in a moment.

First, we'll do our HASELL checks – you call them out for practice. Now we're going to enter a power off stall straight ahead, but this time, about 5 miles an hour before the actual stall, we will apply full left rudder and hold the control column right back. The nose yaws to the left, and there she goes into a spin to the left. We'll just note our altitude – 5,100 feet. We continue to hold the control column right back and still hold full left rudder. Notice the low airspeed and the rapid descent shown on the Vertical Speed Indicator.

To come out of the spin we use **full opposite rudder**, then pause, before gently easing forward on the control column. As the spin stops, we centralise the rudder pedals, and here we are in a fairly steep dive, with our airspeed increasing. Keeping the wings level, we ease out of the dive, and as we come back up to the horizon, we increase the power to our cruise setting of 2,300 rpm and push the carburettor heat back to cold. We now continue to fly straight and level, resuming a good look out.

If you check the altimeter, you'll see that we lost 800 feet before we recovered, so this emphasises the importance of correct and prompt recovery from any stall situation near the ground. However, we really have to misuse the controls by booting that rudder in as we approach the stall, in order to make it spin, and you've just seen that recovery is quite straightforward.

Let's just re-set our directional gyro against the magnetic compass. Notice that the artificial horizon has also 'toppled' due to the forces imposed on it, and it will take a few minutes to re-erect.

Climb back up to 5,000 feet now, and I'll talk you through a spin. I'll be right with you, (I promise, I promise). When you come to take the test, you'll have to be prepared to do one to the left or the right, so we'll do some of each before we call it a day.

If you ever inadvertently get into a spin and aren't sure which way you are spinning, take a look at the turn needle. If it is to the left, you will be spinning to the left and will need to use right rudder to recover. If it is deflected to the right, you'll need left rudder.

Just run through the HASELL checks again, and then we'll have another one to the left. The sooner you recover, the less height you will lose, so once we are established in the spin, I will tell you to recover. When you are ready then – carburettor heat, power off, just as you did with the stalls, still noticing all those symptoms of the approaching stall. Just before the stall, apply full left rudder, control column right back, keeping the ailerons neutral. That's it, and there's the spin. Notice the turn needle is over to the left.

Recover now – full right rudder, and gently forward on the control column. As the spin stops centralise the rudder – good, and now ease out of the dive, and back up to the horizon. That's fine. Let's climb back up and try one to the right. Notice that you don't use power until you have recovered from the spin and are coming back to level flight, because you are already in a dive at quite a high airspeed. If you ever accidentally spin with power on and flaps down, close the throttle and bring the flaps up. One thing to avoid when you are coming out of the dive is a harsh backward movement on the control column, as this could cause what is known as a high speed stall. Gentle back pressure is all that is necessary.

After this one, we'll head for home. You've had quite a work-out, and your instructor feels sick.

Before you rush off, let's take a look at those airspeeds. The white arc on the airspeed indicator is the flap operating range, the green arc is the normal operating range, the yellow arc is the caution range, and the red line is the 'never exceed' speed. All these are calibrated (rectified) airspeeds.

Indicated Airspeed is the speed you read on the airspeed indicator, usually presented in miles per hour and knots. *Calibrated Airspeed* is used in the handbook on American aeroplanes, and it is the same as *Rectified Airspeed*, which is the British term. This is the indicated airspeed corrected for instrument error and installation error.

True Airspeed is rectified airspeed corrected for temperature and density. When you start cross-country flying, you will need to know your true airspeed, although for practical purposes, the temperature and density will not greatly affect you at the low altitudes you will be flying in this aeroplane. *Ground Speed* is the speed you travel over the ground as a result of the wind. You will still be showing the same indicated airspeed, regardless of a headwind or a tailwind.

13 The circuit pattern

You will spend several hours in the circuit. The first time you will be knitting everything together that you have learned so far, (except stalling and spinning, please), and getting used to the basic pattern.

The standard pattern is 'left hand', but at some airfields you may find you have to do a right hand circuit, in order to avoid noise over built up areas to the left of the take off runway, or perhaps so that you can be slotted in with other faster traffic.

Look at the sketch, and we will go through the circuit. The right hand pattern is the same, except that all turns are made to the right.

After take off, we climb straight ahead to 500 feet. As we pass 300 feet on the climb out, we reduce the power to our normal climb setting of 2,500 rpm, so that the engine doesn't get overheated.

Before making a climbing turn to the left, we look down to make sure we have cleared the airfield boundary. (If we were to climb rapidly to 500 feet, after an overshoot, for instance, and were to make our turn before reaching the boundary of the airfield, we could possibly cut across someone else on their 'Downwind leg'.) Assuming we take off directly into wind, as we turn 'Crosswind', we need to straighten up after slightly less than 90°. We want to make a rectangular pattern over the ground, so if we were to turn exactly 90°, the wind that was on our nose on take off would be pushing us back towards the

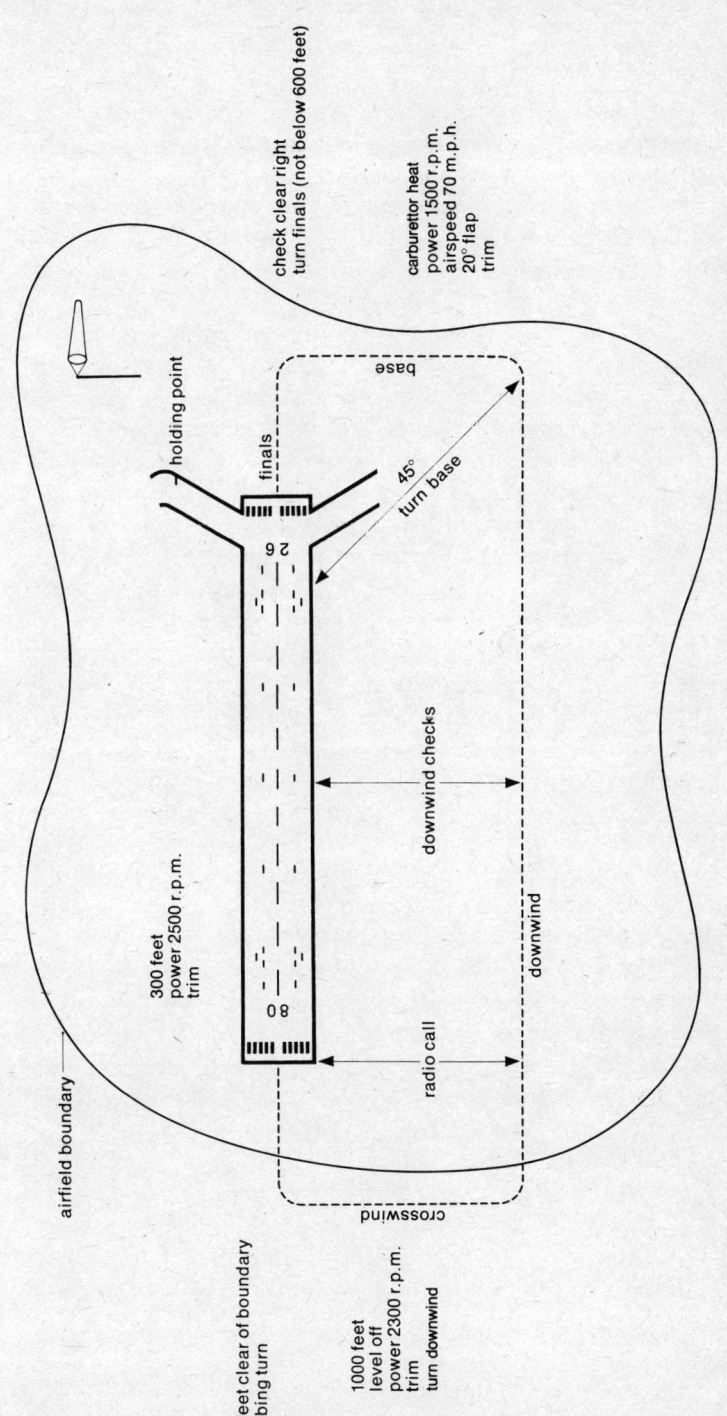

check clear right
turn finals (not below 600 feet)

carburettor heat
power 1500 r.p.m.
airspeed 70 m.p.h.
20° flap
trim

holding point

finals

base

45°

turn base

26

downwind checks

downwind

80

radio call

airfield boundary

300 feet
power 2500 r.p.m.
trim

crosswind

500 feet clear of boundary
climbing turn

1000 feet
level off
power 2300 r.p.m.
trim
turn downwind

The circuit pattern

field, and we would find we had crept in and turned more than 90°. Once we are in the turn, we look down to the left at the end of the runway, and judge the position to straighten up the climb in order to make a square corner.

We climb straight ahead on the crosswind leg until we reach 1,000 feet, and then level off. We now look to the right in case there is another aeroplane joining downwind, then clear ourselves to the left and make a level turn on to the downwind leg. This time the wind is behind us. When we are abeam the end of the runway we have just cleared, we make our 'Downwind' call on the radio.

While flying downwind, parallel to the runway, we do our downwind checks. B (Brakes), M (Mixture), F (Fuel), and H (Harness). We depress the brake pedals and release them, to make sure they are off. We check that the mixture is rich. We check the fuel contents to make sure we have sufficient for an overshoot if necessary. Lastly, we check that the doors are properly shut and that our harness and seat belts are secure. The BUMPFH checks that you may be taught also include U for Undercarriage down and locked, and P for adjusting the Pitch angle of the propeller for landing. Neither of these apply to us, as the undercarriage is not retractable and the propeller pitch angle is fixed on this aeroplane.

Provided we have been cleared to 'finals' by the Tower, we make a level turn on to the 'base leg' when our proposed touch down spot is approximately 45° behind us. We plan to land close to those triangular marks painted on the runway. If you are flying from an airport or field with no obvious markers, wait until the end of the runway is about 45° behind your left shoulder before turning. Once again we want to make a square corner, so we look down and judge when to roll out of the turn. The wind will now be pushing us off to the right, so we need to turn slightly more than 90°.

On Base Leg we set up our approach. We apply carburettor heat, reduce the power to 1,500 rpm, and establish our descent with an airspeed of 70 miles an hour. Next we lower 20° of flap, and then we trim. We will come on to full flap landings later in your training.

Keeping the airspeed at 70 mph, we continue the descent, not turning on to finals below 600 feet. Before we turn, we look to the right to clear ourselves, as there might be someone coming in on a long final unknown to the Tower controller. We then make a descending turn to come out with the runway straight ahead, and we are now on finals.

We will talk about the landing when we are up there, so if you go out to the aeroplane and do a quick pre-flight, I'll book us into the circuit with the Tower.

14 Using the radio

Most people learning to fly have difficulty when starting to use the radio. It is embarrassing not to understand what has been said by the Air Traffic Controller, but only with practice and listening will it fall into place – and bear in mind that everybody, including the controller, has had to learn.

Anticipation of what is likely to be said is half the battle in the early stages of getting your ear used to hearing the message. Don't forget that the whole purpose of using the radio between the pilot and the controller is for communication, so use your own words, (within reason), if you can't remember the correct phraseology. The controller is trying to sort out his known traffic safely, and the pilot is complying with the instructions he receives – a co-operative partnership – so it is very necessary for the pilot to hear and understand what is said. Don't ever feel that rather than query a half-heard or garbled message, you can just say, 'Roger'. In a case like this, ask the controller to repeat the instruction – 'Say Again' – (and again, if you still don't hear it properly). It doesn't matter if you feel a fool, but it does matter if you jeopardize your own and other pilots' safety. Remember that the controller is there to help you.

Let's go through the messages you might expect to hear from start-up to shut-down in the circuit. If you don't already know the phonetic alphabet, now is the time to learn it:

Alpha	Foxtrot	Juliet	November	Romeo	Victor
Bravo	Golf	Kilo	Oscar	Sierra	Whisky
Charlie	Hotel	Lima	Papa	Tango	X-ray
Delta	India	Mike	Quebec	Uniform	Yankee
Echo					Zulu

We'll assume our registration to be G-ABCD. G is the prefix for all UK registered aircraft.

After start-up, allow a few moments for the radio to warm up – don't forget to switch it on. Check that you are tuned to the correct frequency, which will be the Tower when you are on the ground and in the circuit. All frequencies are listed in the COM (Communications) Section of the Air Pilot. Now depress the microphone switch and say,

'Hurn Tower, Golf Alpha Bravo Charlie Delta, Taxy Clearance.'

The Tower will answer and give you first the runway in use and then the altimeter setting(s), so you can expect to hear,

'Golf Alpha Bravo Charlie Delta, cleared to the Holding Point of Runway 26, QNH 1017, QFE 1016.'

You then say,

'QNH 1017, QFE 1016, Charlie Delta.'

It is not necessary to repeat the runway. On the other hand, if you have correctly heard the altimeter settings but didn't catch the runway, now is the time to ask,

'Charlie Delta, Say again runway.'

The controller will repeat the runway for you, and you acknowledge,

'Charlie Delta, 26, Roger.'

You now taxy out to the holding point, and the only other transmission you might receive before you get there is something like,

'Charlie Delta, Caution, there is a Baron crossing you right to left on the taxyway. Taxy behind him to the holding point.'

'Charlie Delta.'

After reaching the holding point, and having completed your checks, you say,

'Charlie Delta, Ready for Take Off.'

You can anticipate one of several replies:

a. 'Roger, Charlie Delta, Hold your position.'(From this you can reasonably assume there is another aircraft on finals, even if you can't see him. As you know, landing aircraft have priority. Possibly there is another aircraft also waiting for take off and the controller wants to get him airborne before you – nothing personal, he's probably been waiting longer.)

b. The controller might say,

'Roger, Charlie Delta, Behind the landing BAC 111, line up and hold.'

A word of caution in such a situation as this. Vortex turbulence behind large aeroplanes can be very severe, and it is advisable to stay clear of it, so you can say,

'Charlie Delta, we'd like to delay take off for a few minutes, due possible wake turbulence.'

The controller is well aware of the hazards to light aeroplanes and will concur with your decision. Remember that this turbulence can float around for some minutes. The same thing occurs when following a large aircraft in to land, so be prepared, and if necessary, orbit or extend your downwind leg until the turbulence can reasonably be expected to have subsided. If you do ever get into such a situation behind a large aeroplane, stay higher than normal on the approach and land after his touchdown point, or if taking off, plan your lift off position after his touchdown point on the runway. However, it is safer to avoid the problem altogether.

Meanwhile, back at the holding point, the Tower might say,

c. 'Roger, Charlie Delta, Line up and hold.'

You would acknowledge this, then taxy out into the centre of the runway and wait for further clearance.

d. The controller might say,

'Roger, Charlie Delta, You are cleared to line up and take off. Wind 270°, less than 5, (which means less than 5 knots), right hand circuits.'

You acknowledge,

'Charlie Delta, Roger, right hand circuits.'

You take off, make your right hand crosswind leg, and turn downwind. Abeam the end of the runway, you say,

'Charlie Delta, downwind.'

Once again, you can anticipate some alternative responses:

a. 'Roger Charlie Delta, Cleared to finals number one.'

b. 'Roger Charlie Delta, You are number three to land. Report before turning base.'

In this case, you would realise there are probably other aircraft on a straight-in approach, or possibly there is another one on a left hand circuit. Always keep an especially good look out for other aeroplanes when you are flying in or near the circuit, as this is where it all happens.

When you are ready to turn on to base leg, you say,

'Charlie Delta, Ready to turn right base.'

The controller may ask you to extend your downwind leg, or possibly, to orbit in your present position. If the visibility is poor, don't extend downwind so far that you lose sight of the airfield, but tell the controller you would prefer to orbit. He will appreciate your reasons and co-operate. However, don't start orbiting without clearance, as there might be someone else following you on the downwind leg. Keep aware of your position as you orbit, remembering that the wind could blow you in towards the runway, or away from it.

If you ever extend downwind so far that you lose sight of the airfield in poor weather – it is unlikely that you will be allowed up on your own in such conditions while you are learning – just remember that when you are cleared to Base leg you will need to turn approximately 90° to the right on a right hand circuit, (90° to the left on a left hand circuit), and then when cleared to finals, turn another 90°, using your directional gyro. Delay setting up the approach, as you can continue at cruise rpm until you are closer to the field again. It won't be long before you see the runway ahead of you, probably off to one side. If you get into this situation and find yourself 'lost', just tell the Tower and they will put you over to the approach frequency. The radar controller will then identify you by giving you headings to steer, and will bring you back to the runway.

Coming back to a run of the mill day, let's say that you are now cleared to turn base. If you are cleared to finals, or not requested to report before turning base, there is no necessity to do so. You do need to report on finals, though,

'Charlie Delta, finals' (or 'Turning finals').
You will then be told,

'Charlie Delta, cleared to land, wind 290, 10.'
This means the surface wind is from 290° at 10 knots, so you will be able to plan your approach. Landing and take off winds are given with the magnetic variation applied to the true wind direction, as runways are aligned with reference to Magnetic North.

If you are told to overshoot, or for some reason decide to overshoot yourself, as you open up the throttle, say,

'Charlie Delta overshooting.'
What is obvious to you in the aeroplane may not be readily apparent to the controller, so don't keep him in suspense.

You will soon get used to the radio. Just think what you are going to say before you start to say it, and you will be able to get your message across. If you begin to say something and your mind goes 'blank', just say,

'Charlie Delta, standby.'
You can then sort yourself out. Take your thumb off the mike button, though, so that others can get in on the frequency while you prepare your speech.

Remember, we have all been through it.

15 Take off, and landing from powered approach

You can call for taxy instructions today, and I'll rescue you, if necessary. If the sound of your voice frightens you, think what it is doing to the controller. He will clear you to the holding point of the runway in use, which will probably be 26, with this westerly wind, and then he'll give you the QFE. I'll jot it down, so if you don't hear it properly, just look at what I've written, and read it back to him. When you are ready, then – Good, let's set the QFE of 1015 on the altimeter and check that it gives us a reading of 0. Now you can taxy out to the holding point, and when you have done your pre-take off checks, you can tell him you are ready for take off.

After you are cleared, double check for unknown traffic on finals, then taxy into the centre of the runway and face in the direction of take off – allow the aeroplane to roll forward a couple of feet to straighten the nosewheel. Look down at the end of the runway and select a reference point to help you keep straight on the take off roll. We'll do the first one together.

Now, with your heels on the floor, to avoid any risk of using the brakes, keep the elevators neutral, and open up the throttle, slowly at first, to give the rudder a chance to be effective, then to full power, holding the throttle in with your right hand. Keep straight with the rudder pedals, and look ahead at your point. You'll need a touch of right rudder during the take off and climb out, due to the effect of the propeller.

As the airspeed increases to 55 miles an hour, ease back on the control column just to take the weight off the nose wheel. As the speed passes 60 mph, move it further back, holding it there, and keep the wings level as we lift off. When we are safely airborne, adjust the attitude to allow the airspeed to increase to 70 mph, and establish the climb. Keep that hand on the throttle during the climb out. Pick yourself another point for keeping straight, as the other one is out of sight below the nose.

As we pass 300 feet, reduce the power to 2,500 rpm and check that you are correctly trimmed for the climb. Continue straight ahead to 500 feet, make sure you are past the airfield boundary, and then clear yourself both ways before entering a climbing left turn on to the crosswind leg – don't let that bank steepen up. Look to your left before continuing with a straight climb – you haven't turned quite enough yet, as we are angling away from the runway, so keep it going a bit longer. Continue now to 1,000 feet and level off. Attitude, power back to 2,300 rpm, and a little forward trim.

Before we turn downwind, look each side of the aeroplane.

We are now abeam the end of the runway, so we say,

'Charlie Delta, downwind.'

The Tower reply,

'Roger, Charlie Delta, cleared to finals number two. Report before turning base,'

so we acknowledge,

'Charlie Delta.'

Just look over to the left and note the distance we need to be out from the runway on our downwind leg. Try to keep at 1,000 feet. If you are too high or too low by 100 feet, you can get back to circuit height by lowering or raising the nose, but if you allow an error of 300 feet to creep up on you, you will also need to reduce the power slightly if you are too high, or increase it if you are too low. Once you are back at 1,000 feet, return to your normal straight and level setting, and re-trim. Perhaps this wasn't quite right at the end of your level off. Meanwhile, as we see-saw on our way, let's do the downwind checks – Brakes, Mixture, Fuel, Harness.

We are coming up to the base leg position now – our touch down spot is about 45° behind your left shoulder – so we'll give the Tower a call, as they wanted us to report before turning, and remember, we are number two in traffic, so keep a good look out for the other aircraft.

'Charlie Delta, ready to turn left base.'

The controller has replied,

'Charlie Delta, cleared to turn left base. You are number two to an Aztec on a right base. Do you have him in sight?' – Do you see him? Yes, there he is, so we say,

'Charlie Delta, affirmative.'

The Tower reply,

'Roger, Charlie Delta, with him in sight, you are cleared to finals, number two.'

We acknowledge this, and make a level turn to the left on to base leg, adjusting our heading for the wind.

We now set up the approach – carburettor heat, power back to 1,500 rpm, 70 miles an hour, then 20° of flap, and trim. There goes the Aztec past our nose on finals, so we know we can continue the approach. Keep your airspeed at 70 miles an hour with the elevators, and control the rate of descent with the throttle.

Remember, we don't want to turn on to finals below 600 feet, so if we are losing height too quickly on base, we add some power.

Coming up to finals, we clear ourselves to the right, then make a descending turn to the left. Watch your airspeed now lower the nose to get back to 70 miles an hour. As we straighten up towards the runway, we report,

'Charlie Delta, finals,'

and they reply,

'Charlie Delta, cleared touch and go, wind 260 at 10 knots. Make it a right hand circuit next time.'

We acknowledge,

'Charlie Delta, Roger, right hand circuit.'

Keeping the airspeed at 70 mph, we continue our approach, with the runway directly ahead of us. If we have moved off to the right, turn the aircraft back to the left, and straighten up so that the runway is on our nose again.

Our touchdown mark should appear in the same position on the windscreen the whole way down – stopping short of actual impact, of course. If it seems to move up, we are too low and undershooting, so provided our airspeed is correct, we will need to add some power to come back to the correct approach path. If our airspeed was too low in this situation, we would need to add considerably more power and if necessary, full power. We can always reduce it again once we are back on the correct descent path at the correct airspeed. If the touchdown point appears to be moving down, we are too high, and will need to increase our rate of descent by reducing the power slightly. Look at the airspeed first, because if this is too low, you will regain 70 mph by lowering the nose, and will also increase the rate of descent. If the airspeed is too high, but the touchdown mark is in the right place on the windscreen, raise the nose to get back to 70 mph, and decrease the power a little to keep the rate of descent constant.

It is very important to keep the correct airspeed on the approach. Too high an airspeed will build in difficulties on landing, and we certainly don't want to stall by letting it get too low. At 70 mph we have a comfortable margin over the stall, but it doesn't take many moments of inattention for that margin to be reduced.

As we come lower, look down ahead of the nose along the runway, so that you learn to judge the round out position. We now check back on the control column a small amount, and take off a little power. Hold that position for a moment while the airspeed reduces and we continue down towards the runway. We now dribble the power off, a little at a time, as we keep easing back on the control column, and about a foot above the runway, we close the throttle completely and the wheels touch down. We land on the main wheels, and try to hold the nose wheel off initially, to avoid wear and tear at this speed, then lower it to the ground, and continue to roll straight down the runway, using rudder as necessary. A very slight amount of rudder at touchdown speeds will produce a large result, so be sparing.

We have been cleared by the Tower for a 'touch and go', so we continue rolling, but before we apply power, we clean up the aeroplane by pushing the carburettor heat back to cold, raising the flaps, and winding the trim wheel forward to the 'take off' position. Don't be in such a hurry to get off the ground again that you forget these things.

We have been cleared for a right hand circuit this time, so as we turn, you will find it a little more difficult to judge your roll out position, because you have to lean over to the right to look down, and in the turn, this high wing blocks your view. However, you know you will need to turn about 90° each time, so use the directional gyro as a rough guide, then stop the turn and correct yourself visually. Your downwind heading has to be approximately 080°, so keep the turn going until then. You may not be able to see the runway, but it will still be there on your right as you roll out, even if it has moved further away, or is at a different angle than you had expected, and you can now adjust your heading so that you are tracking parallel to it.

This time we have been told to extend our downwind leg, because there is other traffic on long finals, so we have a good opportunity to go through a landing without using flaps.

16 More landings

A flapless landing would be used in very windy or gusty conditions, or in the event of electrical failure, because the flaps on this aeroplane are electrically operated. Without using flaps our radius of turn is slightly wider, so we start the turn on to finals a little sooner in order to come out with the runway directly ahead. We also have a flatter approach path, so as we round out above the runway, the amount of back movement on the control column is less, because we are already close to the 'hold off' attitude. Notice that our airspeed falls more slowly and we 'float' a little longer during the hold off period, using up more of the runway – that is why we needed to extend the downwind leg to give us a longer run in on finals. Remember that with flaps up, your stalling speed is higher, so in gusty conditions allow a little extra airspeed on the approach as a precaution.

The surface wind has now veered to 280 at 20 knots. Still using Runway 26, it will be coming between the nose and the starboard wing, so we have to make a 'crosswind' take off and landing. Depending on its velocity (speed), if the wind direction is too many degrees off the runway heading, take offs and landings should not be attempted in light aeroplanes like this. For instance, a surface wind of 310° at 25 knots, gusting 35, would be a strain on both you and the aircraft – to us, it's challenging enough when it's dead on the nose.

With today's wind, as we start our take off roll, we move

	Crosswind Angle								
	10°	20°	30°	40°	50°	60°	70°	80°	90°
	Crosswind Component								
5	1	2	2	3	4	4	4	5	5
10	2	3	5	6	7	8	9	9	10
15	3	5	7	9	11	13	14	14	15
20	3	7	10	13	15	17	18	19	20
25	4	8	12	16	19	22	23	24	25
30	5	10	15	19	23	26	28	29	30
35	6	12	17	22	26	30	32	34	35
40	7	14	20	25	30	35	37	39	40
45	8	15	22	29	34	39	42	44	45
50	9	17	25	32	38	43	47	49	50

(Wind Speed/Knots shown along the left axis)

Example: Take off and Landing Limits

the control column to the right so that the starboard aileron is raised. The wind striking this aileron helps to prevent the wing from being blown up and over. We keep the control column in this position during the whole take off run, delaying our actual lift off a few moments longer than usual, so that we have a slightly increased airspeed.

We now lift the aircraft off positively, momentarily taking off a little right aileron to avoid the risk of touching the starboard wing tip to the ground, and let the airspeed build up to 75 miles an hour. In gusty conditions, that extra 5 miles an hour gives us more positive control. We want to stay over the runway on the climb out, so we keep the control column to the right sufficiently to counteract for the drift. If you look down, you will see that although the aircraft nose is pointed to the right, we are actually tracking along the runway — with a bit of luck.

We adjust our crosswind leg as necessary, and then turn downwind. The wind will now be blowing us towards the runway, (on a right hand circuit), and we have to head the aeroplane more to the left, so that we track parallel to it.

Coming up to base leg, we know we will have to turn more than 90°, so that we aren't drifted too far from the airfield, and we will need to turn on to finals sooner, so that we don't go through the centreline of the approach. On finals the wind is blowing on our right side again, as it was during the take off.

There are two methods of landing crosswind. One is to keep the nose of the aeroplane lined up with the runway, but have the right wing down into the wind, (control column to the right), using sufficient opposite rudder to keep straight. Allow a slightly higher airspeed on the approach if the wind is strong, and keep positive control. Don't let a lull in the wind allow you to relax your wing down attitude, as a sudden gust near the ground might flip the wing up if you are holding the control column too slackly. Be prepared for turbulence if you pass over hangars or thick woods shortly before the runway.

Make a normal powered approach, and don't be in a hurry to start bringing the power off. Make sure you are over the end of the runway before you check back and start the round out, still keeping that right wing down and using left rudder to keep straight. The aileron is held on during the hold off and touch down – a sensible amount, remembering that right wing tip. With this cross wind landing method, you actually touch down on one wheel and the other one then settles to the runway. During the landing run, the aileron is still held into the wind.

The other crosswind landing technique involves 'crabbing' after turning on to finals, by pointing the nose into wind so that the aeroplane is drifted back to the centre line of the approach path as you descend. If the wind is from the right side of the runway, look to the left of the nose and keep yourself, (not the aeroplane), lined up with the approach. You can then judge the amount you need to turn into wind in order to keep the aircraft tracking in a straight line towards the runway. Just before touch down, it will be necessary to yaw the aeroplane round with opposite rudder, so that it lands facing straight down the runway. If the wind is strong, be prepared to stop that right wing being flipped up by moving the control column to the right, and then once you are down, continue the landing run with right aileron held on.

Let's go round again and have some more practice. Tell me which method you plan to use each time, and then stick to it.

The aircraft ahead has been given a different wind – did you pick it up? The Tower have just said to us,

'Charlie Delta, make this an overshoot. Reposition downwind left hand for 35. Surface wind 320 at 10 knots.' We acknowledge,

'Charlie Delta overshooting to position left hand downwind for 35.'

Open up the throttle to full power, not forgetting a touch of right rudder, push the carburettor heat knob back to cold, and establish our climb attitude and airspeed. Remember to wind the trim wheel forward. As we pass 200 feet, you can raise the flaps. Continue climbing straight ahead, correcting for the wind so that we track along the runway. When we are through 300 feet, ease the power back to 2,500 rpm and check the trim. For future reference, you would overshoot at any time that you are not happy with the approach. If you come in too high, or the round out doesn't seem quite right, or an elephant lumbers across the runway, promptly apply full power and go round again.

Now let's think what we have to do today. We will be landing on 35, and remember, that is 35(0)° – a northerly direction. As we overshoot, we are heading to the west, so if we turn to the left we will be heading south, (170°), and will be downwind for 35. We will actually be further along the downwind leg than if we had just taken off on 35, so will report,

'Charlie Delta, downwind left hand 35,'
and do our downwind checks. If you are ever instructed to change runways, just work out the downwind direction, then look at your present heading, and you will know whether you have to turn to the left or the right. It helps if you can visualise the points of the compass.

As we continue downwind for 35, the wind will be drifting us to the left, in towards the runway, so we must correct by heading slightly to the right. Turning on to base leg, the wind will be blowing us away from the field to the right unless we correct by crabbing more to the left. You will soon learn to judge how much to turn by looking at the runway and making yourself think about the wind direction. Which way will you need to correct on finals for 35 with a surface wind of 320°?

Next time round we will make a glide approach, so instead of bringing the power back to 1,500 rpm when we start the descent, we will close the throttle completely – this is the type of landing you would do if your engine failed. You will have a complete lesson on forced landings later on, so this will be good practice for you to judge the direction and strength of the wind, which is now 340° at 15 knots.

We'll start the base leg a little closer to the end of the runway than for a powered approach, because we are going to close the throttle before turning. We have been cleared to finals, so we can set up the approach at the end of the downwind leg. That's it, and now let's lower 10° of flap. When we have turned base we can assess the strength of the wind and see how it affects our rate of descent. If we find we are losing height too quickly, we'll start our turn to finals earlier. If we are a little high we can put down some more flap and we can also turn a few degrees away from the runway while we lose height. Remember to warm the engine.

We'll start our turn to finals before we come level with the runway, as the wind will drift us across to the approach path as we turn. Don't forget to clear yourself to the right before turning. Let's have another 10° of flap. It looks as if 20° will be about right this time. Just tell the Tower we are on finals.

With this nose-down attitude, as we come over the runway, we need to check back on the control column a little earlier to establish our hold off attitude. Now, keep coming back, a bit more, hold it there – and THUD, we're down. Put your teeth back in and we'll go round again. As they aren't so busy now, we'll request a right hand circuit, so that you can do one with the wind from the other side of the runway.

As we turn right base the wind will be blowing us away from the runway, so we'll delay lowering the flaps. Ah, too late – never mind, leave them down and we'll see how it works out. Don't put any more down though. With the wind against us, we will need to go right up to the extended centreline before we turn on to finals. If we find we are losing height too quickly, which we are, we can angle in a little, as long as we still leave ourselves a reasonable distance for a straight approach before landing. Remember to report on finals.

Carry on towards the runway. If you think we aren't going to make it, resist the temptation to raise the nose to try and 'stretch the glide', as this will actually increase the rate of descent and your airspeed will be too low. If you are undershooting, use the throttle. Don't leave it too late, as you will contine to sink until the power has a chance to 'bite' and arrest the descent. Good. We'll have a normal powered approach and landing now. There's no point in concentrating so hard on a glide approach that you forget basic common sense, which is to get the aircraft safely on the ground.

As we climb away next time, we are going to simulate engine failure by closing the throttle, so that you will know what to do if you are ever unlucky enough to experience this 'for real' after take off. I'll just tell the Tower what our plans are so that they don't get excited and precipitate crash drill.

Here we are at 300 feet, and we have engine failure. Lower the nose to maintain your gliding airspeed of 70 miles an hour and look straight ahead for a place to land, while you check that the throttle is properly closed and adjust the trim. There's a small field just to the left of the nose and we'll take that. Delay putting flaps down until you are certain you will make the field. Check that your harness, and mine, is secure. If this were an actual engine failure, you would now turn off the fuel and the magneto switches, and open the cabin door a crack, to prevent it jamming on landing. Maintain your airspeed. Good. We'll climb away now – full power – and continue in the circuit. The important rule is 'never turn back towards the runway.' You don't have enough height and airspeed just after take off to allow you to turn downwind safely.

This time we'll go through the type of landing you would use for a short runway. We do a normal powered approach and plan our touch down point at the beginning of the runway – but not before it – bringing the aeroplane to a stop after a short run.

On base leg we lower 30° of flap and trim for the descent at 65 mph. Once we are on finals, we lower the last 10° of flap and maintain an airspeed of not less than 60 mph. (In windy conditions keep it at 65 mph.) We now have a steep nose down attitude and a good rate of descent. Keep the beginning of the runway in the same position the whole way down and don't hesitate to open up the throttle if you are under-shooting. Avoid dragging it in low over the ground.

With full flap we allow the aeroplane to come a little lower before starting the round out and then progressively check back on the control column as we ease off the power. As we close the throttle, the wheels touch down almost immediately and we lower the nosewheel to the ground, then very gently start applying the brakes. Once we have slowed down suf-ficiently, we can use more brake until we stop.

We'll do just one more circuit before going in, so when you are ready we can start the take off roll from here. With any of your landings, if you misjudge your height and close the throttle too soon, you will sink in a flat attitude towards the runway. This is when you must open up the throttle a small amount to 'cushion the blow', or else apply full power and go round again. A short field landing would not normally be expected of you during your initial training and it is more important to concentrate on a good, safe touch down well inside the end of the runway.

The visibility is getting poor now, so we'll keep our downwind leg closer in to the runway. We don't want to lose sight of it, and the controller doesn't want to lose any of his traffic. As the cloud is lowering, we'll reduce the circuit height to 900 feet, or 800 feet if necessary, and make this our landing run.

Next time you come, we'll leave the circuit, and go on to something else.

Congratulations on going 'solo'.

17 Steep turns and more radio

We will be going out to the local flying area again this morning, so shortly after take off, you can anticipate the Tower saying,

'Charlie Delta, continue now with Hurn Approach on 118.65.'

You acknowledge,

'118.65, Charlie Delta.'

You already have the Tower frequency of 118.4 set, so just need to move the small knob to .65. Listen out before transmitting, then say,

'Hurn Approach, Golf Alpha Bravo Charlie Delta.'

As this is the first time on a new frequency, you use the full call sign. The Tower will have told the Approach controller that you are coming to him, so he will probably say something like,

'Charlie Delta, continue as cleared. Report leaving the Zone.'

On the other hand, he might say,

'Charlie Delta, go ahead.'

In this case you would say,

'Charlie Delta just airborne from Hurn, climbing to 1,500 feet, heading to the west.'

When we get to the boundary of the Zone, you can give him a call and say,

'Charlie Delta, clearing the Zone at Poole Harbour, 1,500 feet.'

You can expect to hear,

'Roger, Charlie Delta. Report before re-entering, Portland 1012.'

He is referring to the Portland Regional altimeter setting (QNH), which is the lowest forecast pressure for the region. There are thirteen Altimeter Setting Regions in the United Kingdom. While flying in the Portland Region, which extends for many miles, as you can see on the map, if you have 1012 set on the altimeter, you will have altitude above mean sea level shown. The aerodrome QNH is the setting you put on the altimeter prior to take off and when you are re-joining, giving you altitude above mean sea level in the immediate vicinity of the airfield. Don't get confused.

I'd like you to climb out to the northwest, to get away from the turbulence of this cumulus build up, and then level off at 3,000 feet. Today we'll do some steep turns, with a higher angle of bank than you have used so far. If we increase the bank, we are going to turn faster, so a steep turn would be used for avoiding action. By keeping a good look out at all times, you should be able to see any other aeroplanes in plenty of time to alter course with a medium angle of bank, but in case you ever need to turn quickly, we'll go through the correct procedure.

We'll maintain 3,000 feet, and start with one to the left, so first make sure we are clear all round. We now enter the turn in exactly the same way as a medium turn, but as we come up to the medium angle of bank we increase it to about 45°, and also add a little power to compensate for the extra drag of the higher banked attitude. Because of this extra drag, we need to ease back on the control column so that we maintain our altitude.

We still want to have a balanced turn, so bring the ball back to the centre. Keeping the bank constant with the ailerons, continue looking out to the left as you turn, and note the position of the nose on the horizon. Now glance back at the altimeter. If you are too high, lower the nose slightly. If you have lost a few feet, take off a little bank so that you get more lift and regain 3,000 feet. If you are 200 feet too low, still take off some of the bank, adjust your altitude with the elevators, and then put the bank on again. Avoid pulling back on the control column with a steep angle of bank, as this will simply tighten the turn, and remember, our stalling speed is higher with a high angle of bank.

Look at the directional gyro for a moment, and notice that we have a good rate of turn. (A normal 'Rate One' turn is 3° a second – 360° in two minutes.)

As Brownsea Island shows up well today, we'll use that for

coming out of the turn. Just before we get there, start taking off the bank, and as you come through the medium bank angle, reduce the power to normal cruise rpm, easing forward on the control column as you come back to straight and level at 3,000 feet – give or take.

Let's try one to the right now – remember, the nose will appear in a different position on the horizon. You are losing height, so take off a little bank, and then raise the nose. That's better. I'll just show you what happens if we continue to pull back without taking off the bank first. I'm not going to stall it, but I'd like you to look at the airspeed indicator and note that the airspeed is quite high when the stall warner starts sounding. There it goes, so we reduce the bank and lower the nose a fraction. Now we can ease back to our correct height before increasing the bank again. Try another one to the left.

Now we'll do a couple of turns using 60° of bank. The procedure is the same, but we need to increase the power still further as we put the bank on. Although we are turning faster, we are also increasing the 'loading' on the wings, making our stalling speed even higher. For your test, you will probably only be required to turn at 45° of bank, which is quite sufficient for any normal flying, but have a bit of practice at 60° turns until you are happy with them – or they are happy with you. Remember to come back on the power and ease the nose forward as you level out.

Let's head back to the field now. As we come up to the Zone boundary, check that the Approach frequency is clear, then say,
    'Hurn Approach, Golf Alpha Bravo Charlie Delta'
and wait for them to answer,
    'Golf Alpha Bravo Charlie Delta, Go ahead'
You now go in with your message,
    'Charlie Delta, re-entering the Zone to the north of Wimborne, 1,500 feet. Request joining instructions.'
They answer,
    'Roger, Charlie Delta, cleared VFR to the field, to join right base for 17. QNH 1016, QFE 1015. Report the field in sight.'
You acknowledge,
    'QNH 1016, QFE 1015, for right base 17, Charlie Delta.'
    We can now use a good mnemonic to help us remember the Airfield Approach Checks.

F – *Fuel*
Check contents

R – *Radio*
Correct frequency

E – *Engine*
Mixture rich, and
Check temperature and pressure gauges

D – *Directional Gyro*
Just re-set that. It has precessed about 5 degrees. Hold the aircraft level while you take the reading from the magnetic compass

A – *Altimeter*
Set the Airfield QNH of 1016

When you are quite sure you can see the airfield, say,
        'Charlie Delta, field in sight.'
They say,
        'Roger, Charlie Delta, continue with the Tower now on 118 decimal 4.'
You read back,
        '118.4, Charlie Delta.'
We are heading in a southeasterly direction and plan to land on 17. We have been cleared to join on a right base, so we won't be doing a downwind leg to the north. There is the runway, angling away from us, so carry on in this direction a little longer, and then turn to the left so that we are positioned for right base. Continue the descent to 1,000 feet and level off. You can now set the QFE for landing – 1015. Meanwhile, give the Tower a call,
        'Hurn Tower, Golf Alpha Bravo Charlie Delta, positioning for right Base, 17.'
They have replied,
        'Roger, Charlie Delta, report right base. You are number two to an Islander, presently on a left base. Check the QFE now 1014.'
You say,
        '1014, Charlie Delta.'
Re-set the altimeter, and you can now do the checks that you would normally do on the downwind leg. The Islander is just turning finals – do you see him? This is about the position where we would normally have completed the downwind leg, so you can give the Tower a call,
        'Charlie Delta, joining right base.'
Wait for a moment, and then give them another call. Check the microphone plug and the volume, and I'll do my good deed for the day and change the fuse. It looks as though we

have radio failure, so continue on Base leg and set up your approach. We have already been cleared to finals behind the Islander, and the controller will realise we have a radio problem when we don't answer him. It is possible that he is able to hear us, so as you turn finals, you can say,

'Charlie Delta, transmitting blind, turning finals.'

As we approach, look over at the Tower and anticipate a steady green light, which will clear you to land. There you are, so let's have another of your good landings. Take a quick check of the wind sock so that you know where the wind is coming from.

Now that we are down, what would it have meant if you had seen a steady red light from the Tower just now? That's quite a good answer, but it's not the right one.

Extract from your aviation law book:

Signal	Meaning to aircraft on the ground	Meaning to aircraft in the air
Intermittent green luminous beam	Authorises movement on the manoeuvring area and apron	Aircraft to return to the circuit, or remain in the circuit, at normal circuit height and to await signal for permission to land
Continuous green luminous beam	Authorises take off	Authorises landing
Intermittent red luminous beam	Aircraft to move clear of landing strip immediately	Requires that, owing to aerodrome being unfit or for any other reason, a landing should be made elsewhere
Continuous red luminous beam	Movement on the movement area is prohibited	Requires aircraft to give way to other aircraft and continue circling
Intermittent white luminous beam	Requires return from the movement area to the starting place	Requires aircraft to land at the aerodrome and proceed to the apron
Red pyrotechnic light or red flare (Not directed at the aircraft)		Prohibits aircraft from landing for time being. Cancels any previous permission to land

18   Forced landings

All aeroplanes have to be well maintained and regularly inspected by law, so provided you have done proper engine checks before take off, and periodically while flying, (and remembered to give it some fuel), it is unlikely that your engine will fail. However, we have to make sure you know what to do if ever the need arises, so today we will practise some forced landings. We won't actually land out there, but will come down to a safe height and then overshoot.

We will leave the Zone and climb to 2,000 feet, which is an average height for your cross-country flying in this area. When I close the throttle, the first thing to do is establish the normal glide at 70 miles an hour, and trim. While doing this, we look for a place to land. Open flat fields are not usually thoughtful enough to position themselves nearby, so we'll have to do the best we can in the immediate area, avoiding obviously marshy ground, and meadows with fences across them, bordered by power lines. We'll also avoid flying low over houses and cattle.

We want to land into wind if possible. If there is no bonfire or chimney smoke to give us a guide, we'll remember the surface wind at take off, or failing that, will certainly remember the runway we have just used. If we took off on 08, the surface wind would be from the east, so by turning downwind when the engine fails and flying to the west, it would make it easier to plan an approach back into wind. If there is no appreciable wind, we can select an approach direction that will give us the longest landing run.

Next we will pick ourselves a clump of trees or the corner of a field as a marker for starting our turn on to base leg. We want to arrive over this point at 1,000 feet, so we must have a rough idea of the height of the terrain. It is no great problem when we are close to sea level, but if the ground rises to 500 feet, we will need to be at our marker at 1,500 feet, so that we clear the ground by 1,000 feet. We obviously can't be too exacting about the altitude and will have to use our judgment and common sense when we get out there – so we are doomed before we start.

All the things we have talked about so far will not take long to do in the air and we will have time to check for the possible cause of the engine failure – ignition switches on Both, fuel contents, mixture rich, carburettor heat on, (in case carburettor icing was the problem), oil pressure and temperature. Positively go through each of these items, as you will lose very little height in the few seconds it takes to check them.

With the engine idling, remember to open up the throttle every 500 feet to clear the plugs. In a real situation, of course, the throttle would remain firmly closed. Once you are definitely committed to a landing, give a quick call on the radio,

'Mayday, Mayday, Mayday, Golf Alpha Bravo Charlie Delta, engine failure, attempting forced landing approximately ten miles northwest of Poole harbour.'

Use your common sense on the radio call, bearing in mind that the important thing is to get the aeroplane down safely, (and you with it). Don't spend valuable seconds trying to remember the correct sequence of a Mayday call while you neglect your planned landing, but do try to croak out your call sign, the problem, and roughly where you are, so that the Search and Rescue people can find you as soon as possible.

At the 1,000 foot marker, or before if necessary, turn on to base, which can be varied by angling in towards the field if you are losing height too quickly, or turning out a few degrees if you are too high. Delay lowering the flaps until you are sure of making the field. If you ever had an actual dead engine, you would be losing height faster than in practice sessions with the engine idling.

Coming in on finals, do your normal pre-landing checks. If it was a real emergency, you would also turn off the ignition and the fuel and unlatch the cabin door.

If you ever have to make a forced landing, don't forget that you are still responsible on the ground, and can't wander off to the nearest pub to celebrate your safe deliverance before

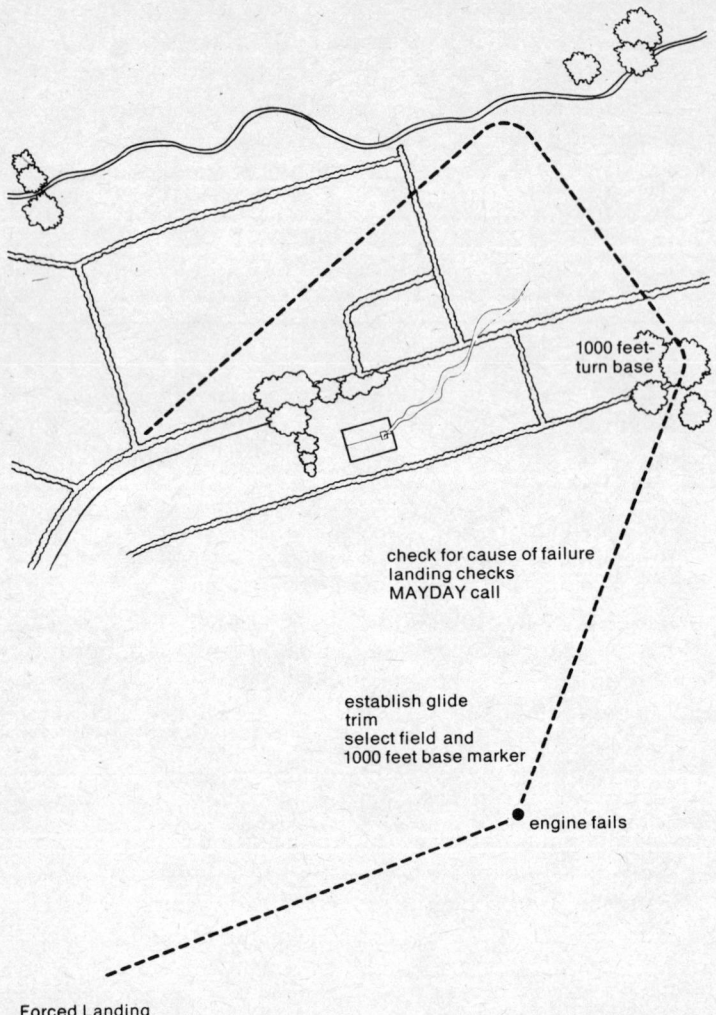

1000 feet-
turn base

check for cause of failure
landing checks
MAYDAY call

establish glide
trim
select field and
1000 feet base marker

● engine fails

Forced Landing

notifying the police and the flying club, and making sure the aeroplane is properly tethered and guarded.

Let's see how it goes, now that we are up here at 2,000 feet, with a reasonable selection of fields. We'll have a good look around for other traffic before we start, and of course, while we are practising, we will avoid other aeroplanes, even if it means opening up the throttle and discontinuing a landing – that will be the one that would have been perfect.

Here we go then – I've closed the throttle and we have engine failure.

First, establish the glide – 70 miles an hour – and trim. Now, look for a field, on either side of the aeroplane. Think about the wind. We took off on 08, but the surface wind we heard on take off was actually 060° if you remember, so turn on to a southwesterly heading – 240° is downwind. Which field are you taking? Good. Plan your approach and pick out a 1,000 foot base marker. As you can continue towards it, check your ignition switches, mixture, fuel, carburettor heat and engine gauges. This is when you would make your Mayday call, so you can say it to me for practice. Don't forget to warm the engine.

We're coming up to your marker now at 1,200 feet, so you have a little height in hand, which is good. Turn on to base, and continue with a normal glide approach. You could put down a little flap. Watch the airspeed. Judge when to turn finals. It's looking good. Do your pre-landing checks. You would have made that field easily, so overshoot now and climb straight ahead to 1,500 feet. Remember not to bring those flaps up until you are well clear of the ground.

We'll do a few more, starting from different altitudes. Don't despair if they don't all work out – it takes a lot of practice. The important thing is to drill yourself in the sequence of priorities. Get in the habit of remembering the wind direction, and noticing good forced landing fields while you are flying.

If your engine ever caught fire, you would promptly close the throttle, lean the mixture, and turn off the fuel. You would also close the cabin hot air intake. Then, with steely nerves, you would plan a forced landing, sideslipping the aeroplane to keep the flames from obscuring your view by holding one wing down and using opposite rudder, keeping the airspeed at 70 miles an hour. Once the engine had stopped, you would turn off the ignition and not attempt a re-start. Fortunately most of us have never experienced this sort of excitement and we're not going to get the matches out now to add realism.

Now let's look at a precautionary landing. One day bad weather or lack of fuel might make you decide to land before reaching your destination, although proper checking of weather and fuel requirements should make it unnecessary. This time you do have power available, so will be able to fly at 200 feet over your selected field to check for holes, fences and other obstructions. You will then climb up to circuit height and fly a standard pattern before making a landing. Once you are down, stay down – don't push your luck. After this overshoot, we'll head back.

We have been given a straight in approach for 08, so we will be lined up with the runway all the way in. This will give you a chance to judge when to reduce the power and start your descent from 1,000 feet. Meanwhile, you can do all your approach and pre-landing checks.

19 Map reading and instrument appreciation

Next time you will be starting cross country flying, so today we will concentrate on accurate headings and maintaining altitude while you divide your attention between the map and the ground. We will take the hood along, so that you can see what it is like to fly in cloud, but always check the weather forecasts thoroughly, because you will need a lot more training before being allowed to fly in instrument conditions.

We'll just have a quick word about the aircraft instruments before we take off. You are already familiar with most of them.

The airspeed indicator works on a differential pressure from the pitot tube and the static vent. The altimeter and vertical speed indicator operate on a difference between pressure from the static vent and the pressure that is in the instrument case.

Today you will use the directional gyro to maintain your headings, and this has to be set against the magnetic compass. The directional gyro is subject to 'precession', but once set it should not differ from the heading on the magnetic compass by more than 3° in fifteen minutes. With a high angle of bank, it is also liable to 'topple', as it did when we were spinning the other day, and will have to be re-set. Apart from these limitations, it is a good heading indicator and much better for navigation than the magnetic compass, which not only reads erratically in turbulent conditions, but also has errors due to 'magnetic dip', which you have probably read about in the books.

If your directional gyro becomes unserviceable you will have to rely on the magnetic compass, so we will use it for one or two turns today. Try to remember a couple of mnemonics – UNOS (Undershoot North, Overshoot South) and ANDS (Accelerate North, Decelerate South). When using the magnetic compass at this latitude, we have to undershoot the heading by about 30° when turning to the north, and when turning to the south, overshoot by the same amount. If you are on an easterly or westerly heading and you increase power and accelerate, the compass will momentarily indicate a turn to the north, and if you decelerate it will indicate a turn to the south.

Because the magnetic compass oscillates, you will find it easier to use if you remember that a standard rate turn is 3° a second. If you want to turn from a heading of 090° to 180° (90°), divide 3 into 90 and turn for 30 seconds. You can then make small adjustments back to your required heading.

Now let's take a look at the artificial horizon. If you ever make the mistake of flying into cloud, the small aeroplane will show you your attitude. Believe what it tells you, even if it shows one wing down and you are convinced you are in level flight. Sight is the only reliable sense in this situation, so ignore all other sensations and bring that wing up level with the horizon bar. If the small aeroplane is above the bar you are climbing, and if it is below the bar you are descending. This is a gyro instrument which is subject to toppling with excessive angles of pitch and bank.

Both the artificial horizon and the directional gyro are operated by suction derived through an engine driven vacuum pump on this aeroplane, which is why we check the suction gauge for sufficient suction during our pre-take off checks.

We have one other gyro instrument, and this is the turn needle, (or small aeroplane on a turn co-ordinator). This is electrically operated and not subject to toppling, so if the artificial horizon and the directional gyro become unreliable, you will still be able to make turns using the turn needle.

In the same instrument case, we have the slip indicator. The ball moves in the curved glass tube through gravity. If you are banked to the left and the ball is to the left of centre, you are in a slipping turn, and if you are banked to the left and the ball is to the right of centre, you are in a skidding turn.

When you are flying, periodically check the ammeter for

positive charge. If you ever had electrical failure, there would still be about thirty minutes of battery power available, giving you time to land at an airfield. It would be important to reduce the load on the electrical system by switching off all unnecessary equipment. You could also notify Air Traffic Control that you would be switching off your radio until just before joining for landing. If you decided to turn off the master switch, remember that your electrically operated flaps couldn't be used, and also that the turn needle would be unusable in a few minutes, after the electric gyro had run down. (Turning off the master switch will not stop the engine, which is independently operated through the ignition system.)

We'll just talk about the VOR, since this aeroplane is equipped with one, but you won't be using it until after your flying test, because it is first necessary to learn navigation without the use of any aids. You will need to be thoroughly checked out on the VOR before using it, so that there is no possibility of misinterpreting the indications.

Look at the map, and just to the northeast of Hurn, you will see a compass rose aligned with Magnetic North. The name of the VOR is written above the square box in the centre, and the I, B and Y of Ibsley are underlined. These are the letters that are transmitted in Morse code, so that you can identify the station. There is also a frequency in the box, but always check in the COM section of the 'Air Pilot' for all frequencies you plan to use, and also check the NOTAMS, which may show not only a frequency change, but also a temporary withdrawal from service of a VOR.

During our pre-take off checks, we dial in the frequency of Ibsley and turn up the volume. Here is the Morse code, so we can jot down the code for I, B and Y, and listen for each letter in turn, to make sure we are tuned to the correct VOR.

A	·—	H	····	O	———	V	···—
B	—···	I	··	P	·——·	W	·——
C	—·—·	J	·———	Q	——·—	X	—··—
D	—··	K	—·—	R	·—·	Y	—·——
E	·	L	·—··	S	···	Z	——··
F	··—·	M	——	T	—		
G	——·	N	—·	U	··—		

Now we centre the needle by rotating the dial. With a 'FROM' indication in the small window and the needle centred, by reading under the pointer we can find out which radial we are located on from the VOR, and can then look at the map and compare this with the bearing of the airport from the VOR. You would use the same tuning and identification method while flying, and can establish which radial you are on from the VOR, regardless of your heading. To fly TO the

VOR, rotate the dial, so that the reciprocal heading is shown under the pointer, with a TO indication in the window. If the needle is centred, you are on that radial, regardless of your heading. If it is to the left, you are to the right of the radial, and if it is to the right, you are to the left. Think of your aircraft as the small circle and fly towards the needle, which will centre when you are once again on the radial to the station. Do not attempt to fly to the VOR with a FROM indication showing – you will get lost and confused. You can fly away from the VOR with a FROM indication, on a selected radial, once again flying towards the needle to keep it centred. You will need to sit down with the books and really understand the operation of the VOR, so we won't spend any more time on it now.

After take off today, I'd like you to climb straight ahead to 500 feet, and then make a climbing left turn on to a heading of 245°. Continue on this heading to 1,500 feet and level off. Good, now turn on to a heading of 270°. If you start taking off the bank approximately 10° before you get to 270°, you will find it easier to come out on the exact heading – if 10° is too much, try 5° next time. When you have cleared the Zone, I'll fly the aeroplane for a moment while you look at the magnetic compass.

We are heading west, so as I add power and accelerate, the compass will indicate a turn to the north, and now, as I decelerate, you will see an indication towards the south. The same would apply if we had been heading in an easterly direction. Now we'll make a right turn to the north, but remembering the UNOS rule, we'll stop the turn at 330°, and wait for the compass to settle down. Then we can correct a little to the right and continue on a northerly heading. Still using the magnetic compass, I'd like you to turn right on to a heading of 180°. This time you will have to overshoot by about 30°, so think what heading you will use to come out of the turn. As the compass steadies, make a small correction back to 180°.

As we've been flying for about twenty minutes, we'll check the directional gyro and use that for our headings now. First, level your wings with the outside horizon. Now look at the artificial horizon, which shows that your right wing is down a little, so bring it up level with the bar. Now look at the heading shown on the magnetic compass and compare it with the one we have. They are both reading the same, so this time we don't need to re-set it.

Take a look at the map for a moment, and you will see that we are flying over Wareham. You can identify it by the double track railway running from the Poole area, paralleling the main road to the west. There's a single track line branching off to the southeast just on the western edge of the town, which crosses a river and joins the road to Swanage. There's also a river running through the town into Poole Harbour. Looking to the north, you will see quite a large wooded area, which is marked on your map.

What heading do you think we would need to get from Wareham to Blandford Forum? North is at the top of the map, so just give me a rough estimate, and turn on to that heading. Next time we will be working out accurate headings before we start cross country flying, but today I'd like you to estimate the direction to one or two places, so that you learn to visualise yourself in the middle of the compass rose, facing to the north, and ignoring the aeroplane's present heading. When you have positively identified Blandford Forum, set course for Hurn, and climb to 2,000 feet.

While you put the hood on, I'll fly the aeroplane. Make sure it is comfortable — it rarely is — and that you can see the instruments.

When you are ready, turn right on to a heading of 180°. Use the artificial horizon, not letting the right wing go past that first mark, which is 30°. About 20° is quite steep enough for normal turning on instruments. Look back at the altimeter, and lower the nose a little to lose that 300 feet you gained in the turn. Now try a turn to the left on to a heading of 090°. On this heading, we'll go through a climb together. Increase the power to 2,500 rpm and establish the climb attitude by easing back on the control column a slight amount, so that the small aeroplane is positioned just above the horizon bar. Now crosscheck with the airspeed indicator to make sure we are climbing at 70 miles an hour. Remember to trim and keep the wings level in the climb. Only very small movements are necessary on the controls, holding each adjustment until you see the result. Just before we get to 3,000 feet, level off by lowering the small aeroplane to the horizon bar, then reduce the power to 2,300 rpm. Eliminate the yaw with a little left rudder, just as you do in visual conditions. Good, now let's go through descending.

Set up the descent in the usual way, holding the small aeroplane on the horizon bar while the airspeed comes back to 70 mph. Now lower the nose slightly so that we maintain our airspeed, and trim. The small aeroplane is just below the bar. Keeping the airspeed at 70 mph, make a descending turn to the right on to a heading of 140°. Not too much bank. Start coming out of the turn a few degrees before 140°. Now continue a straight descent to 1,500 feet and level off.

If you ever run into cloud, go straight on to your instruments and avoid looking outside. If you try to fly 'half and half' you will have problems. If you start to lose control of the situation, look at your airspeed. If it is too low, add power, lower the nose and level the wings on the artificial horizon. If it is too high you are diving, so take off the power and level the wings on the artificial horizon, then ease back up to level flight. Then make a gradual turn in the opposite direction until you are in visual conditions. If you find it difficult to work out reciprocal headings, this may help: if your heading is greater than 200, subtract 200 and add 20. If it is less than 200, add 200 and subtract 20.

I'm just going to see if our friendly Air Traffic Controller can fit us in for a practice Surveillance Radar Approach, so that you will know what to expect if you run into poor visibility and need assistance. He will ask us to make one or two turns for identification on his radar screen and then say,

'Golf Alpha Bravo Charlie Delta, you are identified one zero nautical miles southwest of Hurn. Turn left now, heading 120°. This will be a Surveillance Radar Approach for landing on Runway 26 at Hurn, terminating two nautical miles from touchdown. Obstacle clearance limit one eight zero feet. Check your minima.'

Your minima are your own and your aircraft's limitations on ceiling and visibility. You would be very unwise to descend below 500 feet on final approach if you were still in cloud.

The controller will give you headings to fly and will tell you when to begin descent. Once you are on final approach, he will periodically give you your range from touchdown and tell you the height you should be passing. If you are lower or higher, you will need to adjust your rate of descent with the power to come back to the correct glide path. Acknowledge all heading instructions. If he says,

'Charlie Delta, you are slightly right of the centre line. Turn left heading 255°.'
you say,

'Left 255°, Charlie Delta.'
When he says,

'Charlie Delta, your range is now two nautical miles from touchdown. I cannot assist you further. Continue your approach or overshoot at your discretion,' you look out and should see the runway ahead of you. Tell him that you have the runway and he will tell you to contact the Tower for landing.

You can take the hood off now – I don't trust you to land with it hanging over your eyes.

20 Cross country

You will be doing several cross country trips, some dual and some solo, and whoever flies with you will take you step by step through the planning. You will need a protractor, computer, plotter and map. Make sure the map is current — it's worth the extra money to know there is a new 2,000 foot television mast on your route.

Suppose today we plan to fly from Hurn to Exeter. Before we start planning, we check the weather forecasts for our route, covering the time of our outward trip and for later in the day when we return, to make sure the flight can be completed in VFR conditions.

We now draw a line between the centre of the two airport symbols, (not so thick that it obliterates places we need to identify on the way), and check to see that our proposed route won't take us through any prohibited or danger areas. If it does, we look on the Danger Area Chart, to see if they are active during the time we plan to fly through them — there's nothing quite so active as a firing range. Look along the track line, and a few miles to either side, to check for obstructions and high ground. You can then select a safety altitude for your flight that will give you adequate clearance.

Your instructor will show you how to complete a flight plan form with the details of your flight. If no form is available, you can make one up for yourself on a sheet of paper, including the items shown here.

Destination	Alt.	True Track	TAS	Wind	True Hdg.	Var.	Mag. Hdg.	Dev.	Comp. Hdg.	Dist.	G.S.	Time	ETA	ATA

QNH	QFE

Radio Frequencies

London FIR:	Station	Tower	Approach
Emergency: 121.5			

Fuel Capacity:

Consumption:

Start Up: _____

Shut Down: _____

Flight plan form

We decide to fly at 2,000 feet, which we enter in the altitude column. Now we find out the True Track, by placing the protractor approximately half way along our line and reading off the compass point. If you are using a square protractor, north should be to the top when you place it on the track line. With a semi-circular type, slide it along the line until the small hole is over one of the meridians of longitude, and read the track where this vertical line extends through the curved scale. Be careful to take the correct figures, as the reciprocal direction won't get you where you want to go. We enter the 268° in our True Track column. Using a True Airspeed of 75 knots, we enter this in the next column.

We now look at the forecast sheets from the Meteorological Office, to find out the wind for our proposed altitude. If you are given 340/20 knots for the 2,000 feet wind, and 350/25 knots for the 4,000 feet wind, and planned to fly at 3,000 feet, you would have to interpolate like this:

$$2,000 - 340/20$$
$$3,000 - 345/23$$
$$4,000 - 350/25$$

If it doesn't work out at an exact half, take the nearest whole number. Your flying is not going to be that exact, and there will probably be some difference between the actual and forecast wind. All you can do is work out the flight plan with the best information you have available and then make corrections as necessary when you are up there. Winds aloft are given referenced to True North, and the velocity is given in knots. We will be using the 2,000 foot wind today, so we enter this in the wind column on the flight plan.

Now we take the computer. Most of them are supplied with a handbook with all the instructions. Turn it to the back side, and erase any pencil marks on the perspex which may have been left from a previous trip. To enter the wind, turn the ring until 340° is under the small arrow at the top. Now slide the scale up or down until the centre dot is over one of the heavy lines, so that it is easier for counting. We have a 20 knot wind, so count down below the dot and put a small pencil cross on the second heavy line – (each band contains 10 knots). Now move the scale until the centre dot is over the True Airspeed of 75 knots. You could also work it out in statute miles per hour, but would first have to convert the wind speed and true airspeed to statute miles – easily done on the front of your computer.

Now turn the ring until the true track of 268° is under the index. If you look at the pencil cross, you will see that it has moved 16 degrees left of the centre line, (16° of port drift). Each square is 2°. With this wind, it looks as though we will have to fly 16° to the right, but we'll just check that. We move the dial to the left so that the pointer is over 284°. If we now look at our cross, we see that it has moved to 15° of port drift, so a correction of 16° would have been too much. With a correction of 15°, (283°), the cross stays on the 15° drift line, so this will be our true heading in order to stay on track. Always check that the number of degrees between the true track and the true heading are the same as the degrees of drift.

Looking at the pencil cross again, and reading up from the horizontal arcs, we see that it is positioned between 60 and 70, so we have a speed over the ground (groundspeed) of 66 knots, which we enter on the flight plan.

So far we have been talking about True Track and True Heading, but now we have to take into account the variation between True and Magnetic north. If you look on the map you will see a dashed line running diagonally north-east/southwest half way along our track. Follow the line to the bottom of the map and you will see that it says 8°W. Variation changes over a period of years, and this is another reason why you should always use a current map. There is an easy rule to help you remember whether to add or subtract the variation to your true heading – East is Least, West is Best. As we have 8° West, we add 8 degrees to 283°, and our magnetic heading to Exeter is 291°.

We also have to consider deviation, which is the effect on the magnetic compass of various electrical and metal items in the aeroplane. You have probably noticed that small card in the cockpit with such instructions as 'For 0 Steer 001'. Periodically, the compass is 'swung' on the Compass Base at the airport, and these small corrections are then listed. If we apply deviation to our magnetic heading, we get compass heading. Always be careful not to place metal objects close to the magnetic compass when you are flying.

Next, we measure the distance between the two airports. If you don't have a plotter showing nautical miles, there is a scale on the bottom of the map. You could also measure segments of your distance on the vertical scale of the longitudinal line, as each degree of latitude is sixty nautical miles.

Now turn to the front side of the computer and place the small arrow, (rate pointer), under the ground speed of 66 knots. Look on the outside (miles) scale for your distance of 61 miles, and on the inside (minutes) scale, read 55½ minutes, which we will call 56. We'll add two minutes to this time, because our climbing airspeed, (and therefore our ground-speed) will be slightly less than when we are in level flight, and at a rate of climb of approximately 500 feet per minute, it will take us two minutes to climb to 2,000 feet.

If our fuel consumption is 4.5 gallons per hour, we place the rate pointer under 4.5, and over 58 minutes, we read 4.35, which is the amount of fuel we can expect to use on our outward trip. We would actually use more than this, allowing for start up, taxying and waiting at the holding point, so must always allow a safety margin, and enough fuel for a possible diversion – like getting lost.

Now let's pick out some good check points. When you are flying, you will have the map on your knees so that you are looking down the track line towards your destination. About seven minutes after take off, we will pass to the north of Poole Harbour, with the distinctive power station chimneys on our left, and six minutes later we should be able to see that road junction and small town on our port side. Notice there is rising ground between the two roads, with a spot height of 159 feet above mean sea level. (If it was above ground level, the figures would have been in brackets. Look at all the information on the bottom of the map.) After another six minutes we pass to the north of Puddletown, with a small river running through it, and we should now be able to see Dorchester ahead to the left. Twenty-seven minutes after take off, we cross a road, then a railway, and another road northwest of Dorchester, the railway running into a junction on our starboard side, and seven minutes later we should be one mile north of Bridport.

We will then be paralleling the coast road, with Lyme Regis and Seaton on our left. Notice the disused railway running down to Seaton – we should be south of the main line loop. We will now start running into rising ground, and shortly after crossing another disused railway, should see Exeter Airport ahead, with the motorway beyond. We know we have the coast to the south, so it will be difficult to get lost, even for us.

When you are flying inland, try to avoid panicking if you miss a check point. Maintain a steady heading, fly the correct altitude and airspeed, and note your elapsed time since the last check point. If your groundspeed is slower than anticipated, you are probably not there yet. Look ahead on the map for an identifiable feature on either side of the track line. Unless there has been a drastic change in the wind, and provided you have been holding a good heading, it is unlikely that you will be very far off track. If you decide to fly along a railway until you can identify your position, remember to keep it on your left. There is good radar coverage in the United Kingdom these days, and help is available, if necessary, from both Civil and Military controllers, so don't fly blindly on until you run out of fuel and daylight. If you have a problem, tell someone on the ground, and follow their instructions.

When you are flying on a route that crosses a Military Aerodrome Traffic Zone, remember that this extends to 3,000 feet above mean sea level. (Civil Aerodrome Traffic Zones extend to 2,000 feet.) Before entering a MATZ, give them a call, telling them your aircraft type, altitude, present position and heading, and request clearance to cross en route to your destination. If, for some reason, you don't get a reply to your call, climb to at least 3,000 feet until you are clear, to avoid engaging in dog fights with military aeroplanes.

There is some controlled airspace which you are not allowed to enter without a full Instrument Rating, and a fully instrument-equipped aircraft – check your aviation law book. You can usually cross below the base of an Airway, but always look at your proposed route carefully to make sure you don't infringe this type of airspace.

While cross country flying, you can call the London Flight Information Region for traffic information on your route, latest weather, or perhaps the frequency of an airfield, if you are diverting from your original destination due to bad weather. The call sign is 'London', and you would give them your Identification, Type, Position, Altitude, In flight conditions – VMC or IMC, and in your case, be sure you are in Visual Meteorological Conditions – Airfield of Departure, Destination, and True Air Speed. They can only give you known traffic, so don't relax your lookout.

During your flight, remember to check the directional gyro every fifteen minutes, and if necessary, re-set it. At the same time, check the ammeter and the suction gauge, the oil pressure and temperature gauges, the fuel and the rpm. Don't forget the rpm check, because if you have not altered the power setting, and are maintaining a constant altitude, the first warning of possible carburettor icing will be a slight drop in the rpm. When you see this, apply full carburettor heat. You will then see a further drop as heated, thinner air enters the carburettor, and if ice is present, may hear a spluttering sound as it melts. The rpm will then increase again. Return the carburettor heat knob to cold, but if icing conditions exist – sometimes on a warm summer day carburettor icing is possible if the relative humidity is high – monitor the rpm, and don't hesitate to use carburettor heat if necessary.

On a long cross-country flight, with variable winds, you will need to check your ground speed. Note the time over one position, then measure the distance to the next check point and when you come to it, jot down the time. If it takes seven minutes to fly eleven miles, take the computer and place the 11 miles above the 7 minutes. Over the rate pointer read the new ground speed of 94. You can then amend your estimates for the rest of the flight.

Carrying on with our plans for an uneventful flight to Exeter, make a mark on the track line for each of the check points you intend to use, but don't select so many that you cover the map with confusion – we can't have more than two of us confused.

We'll now check the NOTAMS for any recent information that might affect us, and also look through the Royal Flights to see if a Purple Airway has been established anywhere on our route. Then we'll take the 'Air Pilot' and write down all the frequencies we are likely to use, in logical order. We can find out the time Exeter Airport closes by looking in the Schedule of Hours in the AGA section. Still in the AGA section, under Exeter, we can make a note of the runways, elevation, and any other information we might need, such as the grade of fuel available. With full tanks, this aeroplane has approximately four hours of flying time, so there should be no need to refuel at Exeter, even allowing for a diversion. Today, we could return to Hurn as our alternative airfield, unless we anticipate fog coming in along the coast later in the day, when we would divert inland. Fog might form if the forecast showed the temperature and the dew point close together.

Let's make a sketch of the runway directions, so that you will be able to visualise how the landing runway will be aligned in relation to your heading as you approach the airfield.

If, in the future, you decide to file a VFR Flight Plan for any of your trips, you will need to call Flight Clearance at least thirty minutes before you leave, having first completed an official Flight Plan form with the required details from your own flight plan. This morning we'll just book out to Exeter.

We are using Runway 35 today. Jot down the time as we start our take off roll, so that we know when we can expect to be over our first check point. Climb ahead to 500 feet on the runway heading before turning back to the left, straightening up on about 285°, until we re-intercept our track line. If we turned on to our magnetic heading of 291° immediately after take off, we would be flying parallel to, but slightly north of track.

Leaving the Zone, we are given the Portland setting and told to continue with en route frequencies. We acknowledge the QNH, which we set on the altimeter, and correct back to 2,000 feet. Stay listening out on the Approach frequency for a while, both for traffic information, and to give your ears practice in picking up other pilots' transmissions.

We adjust our heading as necessary to stay on track. If we find ourselves over the railway junction northwest of Dorchester, instead of two miles further south, provided we have been holding a constant heading, we can assume the actual and forecast winds are different. Head the aeroplane a few degrees to the left while you work out a corrected heading to Exeter. The 'One in Sixty' rule states that if you are one mile off track after sixty miles, you will be one degree off track. If you find it difficult to apply this rule mentally, you can use your computer. Place the 2 miles off track over the 28 miles flown from Hurn, and opposite the pointer read 4.25. Now place the 2 miles off track over the 32 miles to go to Exeter, and read 3.75. Add the two together and you get 8°. You need to correct to the left, so subtract 8° from 291°, and take up a new heading of 283°.

Ten minutes before we are due to arrive, we call Exeter Approach, so if our ground speed is the same as when we started, shortly after crossing the disused railway line running south to Seaton, we tune in the correct frequency and say,

'Exeter Approach, Golf Alpha Bravo Charlie Delta.'
When they tell us to go ahead, we say,

'Charlie Delta, two miles north of Seaton at 2,000 feet, estimating Exeter in ten minutes. Request joining instructions.'

They have given us the airfield QNH, and told us to position for a straight in approach to Runway 31. By astute planning, impeccable navigation, and a stroke of luck, we see the airfield ahead of us. We haven't been given the QFE, so we say,

'Charlie Delta, field in sight. May we have the QFE,'
and then set this on the altimeter. As we come closer to the field, we will turn slightly to the right to line up with Finals for 31. After landing we'll go over to the building marked with a 'C' to pay the landing fee, and can then have a cup of tea to toast our success.

21 The written exams and the flight test

You will have to take – and pass – written examinations on
Aviation Law, Airframes and Engines, and Navigation and
Meteorology. Towards the end of your training, try to get one
out of the way each time you come to fly. The papers are
'multiple choice' and you have to select the correct answer. If
you can't answer a question immediately, go straight on to the
next one. There is a time limit set for each examination, and
you can come back to those that need more of a pause for
thought when you have at least some certainties in the bag.
Seventy per cent is the pass mark for all the written examinations.

The Aviation Law paper calls for a certain amount of
parrot-fashion learning. Some of the questions may puzzle
you, (especially the ones you get wrong), and you may wonder
why you need to know things that could be looked up when
necessary, but it's not worth failing at this stage, so make the
effort to go through each section of the book, even if you
forget some of it afterwards. Take a look at those pink
Aeronautical Information Circulars too, as there might be a
question from one of them.

Coming on to the Airframes and Engines examination,
most of the questions cover things you need to know for your
own benefit when you are flying with your family and friends.
Your instructor will help you go through the handbook of the
aircraft you fly, and will explain the performance charts and

show you how to work out the weight and balance. If it is an American handbook, the fuel and oil will be given in US gallons, so make sure you know the capacity and consumption in Imperial gallons. Also, check the octane rating that is used where you fly, as it will probably be differently listed in the book. You need to know the baggage capacity, and where the emergency equipment is stowed. You may have one or two questions where you have to apply your knowledge of the instruments and controls on the aircraft – there's always a drawback, isn't there?

On to Navigation and Meteorology. You will be given a map, and will need a protractor, plotter and computer. You can expect several questions about cross-country flying, and will probably be given the co-ordinates in Latitude and Longitude of two airports. If you are asked to plan a flight northwest from a particular location, your True Track cannot possibly be 150°, so don't throw marks away by taking the reciprocal figures from the protractor.

Really read the questions and avoid 'pouncing' on the wrong answer. You might have a question like this:

With a True Track of 270°, Magnetic Variation of 6° West, and 10° of port drift, your Magnetic Heading would be –
 (a) 266°   (b) 274°   (c) 286°

Work it out logically. The wind is blowing you to the left, so you will have to correct 10° to the right it you want to stay on your track line. You add westerly Variation, remember, so the correct choice must be Answer (c). In Answer (a) they have subtracted the 10° drift, so that you would be even further off track to the left, and in Answer (b), they have correctly added the 10° drift, but subtracted the Variation, which would have been the correct answer if it had been 6° East.

In questions where you need to use a computer, select the answer that is closest to yours. Different makes of computers may produce very slight variations when working out a problem, so several types are used when the examinations are set. However, there will only be one correct answer, and the other two will not be close enough to be confused with computer error. For instance, with this choice,

 (a) 263°   (b) 271°   (c) 255°

if the answer you get is 261°, you would select Answer (a), but apply your genius to it again, just to make sure.

Don't forget there is a lot of free information on the map itself. The weather questions will be practical, and you will need to read up on winds, fog formation, icing and turbulence associated with different clouds and frontal systems.

You will have a practice run through before taking the Flight Test, which covers pre-flight, start up, taxying and take off, climbing up to do steep turns, one or two stalls and a spin. You can also expect a forced landing before returning to the airfield for landing, so until you have done this, keep an eye open for a good field, and remember the surface wind when you take off – this way, you will be ahead of the game.

You will probably find the test quite undemanding after all the nagging of the past few weeks, and the Examiner will be very fair to you, so there is no need to ingratiate yourself with him beforehand. You wouldn't be human if you weren't a little nervous, but by the time you've stumbled and stuttered and tried to start the engine without turning on the ignition, he will get the picture and make allowances. He is not necessarily going to fail you if you go to 200 feet too high in the circuit, but he will certainly be waiting to see if you do something about it.

Avoid trying to con him, as he's heard it all before. If you realise you aren't going to make the field on your forced landing, it is better to open up the throttle and say you've made a mess of it, than to insist you would have reached it. He will probably let you have another try, and may even help you with the next one. He will be looking to see how well you overshoot after the forced landing, so don't give up half way. That goes for any mistakes you make. Your flying will get progressively worse if you spend time worrying about something you've done wrong instead of concentrating on the job in hand. Remember, he's not expecting perfection, (though no doubt he's ever hopeful), but he is looking for safety and common sense.

Make the effort to go through the HASELL checks every time you stall and spin. After the first stall, he may decide that you needn't do all the checks again, but leave it to him to stop your recitation if he wants to.

He will expect you to clear yourself before turning and to keep a good look out for other traffic. It's not a bad idea to put your finger on each of the instruments as you check them, so that he can see you are doing it – don't poke his eye out, though.

Avoid frightening him on finals by letting your airspeed get too low. He knows he can take over, but he is testing you to see if you are safe to let loose on the general public, so convince him, and yourself, that you are capable.

If your landing is a bit rough, you can still make the landing run good, clear the runway, and stop while you do your after landing checks, then taxy smoothly back to the hangar and complete your close down checks efficiently. There's a lot more to passing the test than a perfect landing.

If you do fail, find out where you went wrong and arrange to take the test again. There are some very experienced pilots around who have failed various tests during their flying careers, but they have been stubborn enough to keep going, and we won't allow you to give up for a footling reason like not passing the first time – besides, you *are* going to pass –

CONGRATULATIONS!

Before you stagger off into oblivion, remember to check the current requirements for keeping your licence valid.

Bibliography

Try to read as many flying training books as possible. A rather complicated explanation in one may suddenly become clear in another. Those listed below should be helpful to you:

Birch N. H. and Bramson A. E.: *Flight Briefing for Pilots, Vols. 1–4* (Pitman).
Volumes 1 and 4 of particular interest to the private pilot.

Birch N. H. and Bramson A. E.: *Flight Emergency Procedures for Pilots* (Pitman, 1973)
It pays to be prepared.

Campbell R. D.: *Flying Training for the Private Pilot Licence* (Aircraft Owners and Pilots Association, 1976)
Comprehensive coverage of the P.P.L. syllabus.

Edwards, Michael: *The Aviator's World* (David & Charles, 1974)
A general guide, touching on all aspects of aviation. Sections relating to aeroplanes and club flying useful.

Francis, Mary: *A Beginner's Guide to Flying* (Pelham, 1969)
Just what it says, and easy to understand.

Ogilvy, David: *Flying Light Aircraft* (A. & C. Black, 1972)
Good explanations.

Welch, Ann: *Pilot's Weather* (John Murray, 1973)
Everything you need to know about the weather for your flying.

Civil Aviation Authority: *The Student Pilot's Licence and Private Pilot's Licence* (CAP 53)
Includes details of the requirements and examinations for the Private Pilot's Licence.